Leland V. Bell

IN
HITLER'S
SHADOW

THE ANATOMY of AMERICAN NAZISM

National University Publications

KENNIKAT PRESS • 1973

Port Washington, N.Y.• London

Library of Congress Catalog Card No: 72-89991
ISBN:0—8046—9029—4

Manufactured in the United States of America

Am

Published by
Kennikat Press, Inc.
Port Washington, N. Y./London

TO EVELYN

ACKNOWLEDGMENTS

In preparing this book I am grateful to several individuals. I am indebted to the staffs of the Library of Congress, the National Archives, and the New York Public Library for the many ways they aided my research. Dr. William T. Doherty and Dr. Edward M. Steel of West Virginia University offered helpful advice in the initial stages of the project. I express thanks to Dr. Clara Howe, of Central State University, who carefully read the entire manuscript, detecting and eliminating awkward phrases. Finally, I wish to thank my wife, Evelyn, for her encouragement and assistance.

L.V.B.

Yellow Springs, Ohio
April, 1972

CONTENTS

IN
HITLER'S
SHADOW

INTRODUCTION

During the decade of the 1930's great political dramas unfolded in Europe. In Germany, Hitler's capture of power was followed by the inauguration of daring, aggressive domestic and foreign policies which affected a boom economy and made Berlin the focal point of European international affairs. Hitler's audacity was matched to a lesser degree by Mussolini's conquest of Ethiopia, which shattered the League of Nations. The march of fascism was not confined to Germany and Italy but penetrated across the Continent: under Francisco Franco in Spain, Léon Degrelle in Belgium, Ferencz Szalasi in Hungary, Corneliu Zelea-Codreanu in Romania, and Oswald Mosley in England. Liberal institutions everywhere appeared to be crumbling under pressures of fascist leaders.

Apprehensive over the spread of fascism in Europe, Americans viewed with dismay and shock the German-American Bund, the most significant of all American Nazi groups. The Bund reached its high point of power in the mid-1930's, when it tried to nazify the German-American community, and until America's entrance into World War II it was the most publicized extreme right-wing organization in the United States. Newspapers throughout the nation carried dramatic photographs of Bund events and reported its rallies, the statements of its leaders defending the Third Reich, and its general espousal of Nazi ideals. Many of these news stories were exaggerations or distor-

3

tions of facts. For example, it was erroneously assumed that the Bund received direct orders from Hitler, that it embraced a membership of half a million, and that it was preparing a violent overthrow of the government. These reports provoked the gravest concern. As Americans observed Bund spectacles of men garbed in brown shirts and swastika arm bands haranguing mass audiences with Nazi plans of aggression and practicing storm trooper exercises in street fighting, the possibility seemed real that in America, too, fascism might triumph. Representative institutions might break down, and the country might succumb to a dictatorship. Overwrought by the fear that a mass Nazi movement was taking root in the United States, Americans reacted swiftly and hammered the Bund out of existence. It was subjected to a series of investigations and legal suits; veteran groups invaded its meetings; and anti-Nazis countered every Bund rally with an anti-Bund demonstration. By the time federal authorities suppressed it in December 1941, the Bund had become a hollow shell. Its few remaining members engaged in self-pity, bickered with their leaders, and blamed each other for the movement's failure.

American Nazism did not die with the collapse of the Bund in 1941 or with the destruction of the Third Reich in 1945. After World War II it embraced an assortment of groups. Most were small secret organizations which held bizarre rituals. A few were cliques of immature teen-age pranksters who passionately collected Nazi paraphernalia and dabbed swastikas on Jewish synagogues and gravestones. In the late 1940's and early 1950's the National Renaissance Party, led by James H. Madole of New York, aroused short-lived attention with a demand that the United States purge its Jews. But the organization which best typified the neo-Nazi revival was George Lincoln Rockwell's American Nazi Party. It was brazen and unequaled in its vulgarity, but Rockwell was a skillful agitator who knew how to capture publicity. What made the organization appear threatening was that its rise to national attention coincided with the wave of right-wing activity which swept the country during the Kennedy and Johnson administrations.

Bundists of the 1930's and Rockwell's Nazis of the 1960's shared common characteristics. Both aped the outward forms of German Nazism, complete with swastikas, uniforms, and Nazi songs. Their ideology was basically the same: adoration of Adolf Hitler as the savior of mankind, coupled with racism, the root obsession of Nazism. Each Nazi organization believed that the country's problems stemmed from the influence of allegedly inferior races. Bundists parroted Hitler's accusations against Jews, while the neo-Nazis held Blacks as well as Jews responsible for America's troubles. Both aimed their appeals at a large constituency, a vaguely defined group called "white Christian Americans," who, they anticipated, would help them build a National Socialist United States. Both tried to transplant Nazism to America by means of bombastic pronouncements, demonstrations, and dire prophesies. This extremism created fear, divisiveness, and hatred in society and often resulted in violent confrontations between Nazis and their opponents.

1
FRIENDS OF THE NEW GERMANY

Until 1933, when Adolf Hitler moved with terrifying rapidity to create the Third Reich, the Nazi movement in the United States lacked cohesion and direction. Its membership embraced young, rootless German immigrants who either worked independently or joined together in small fringe groups to win sympathy for the party in Germany. At loose ends after the abortive Beer Hall Putsch in 1923, Kurt Georg Wilhelm Ludecke, an ardent, brash Nazi, came to America and engaged in an unsuccessful one-man crusade to secure financial support for the Nationalsozialistische Deutsche Arbeiterpartei (NSDAP). Henry Ford, German-Americans, and the Ku Klux Klan were so unresponsive to his pleas that he correctly called his fund-raising effort an "unprofitable American begging tour."[1] In 1924 other followers of Hitler established a society in Chicago popularly known as Teutonia, the first important expression of organized Nazism in the United States. During the late 1920's Nazi annals record nothing spectacular, and the activities of Teutonia reflected this parlous state of affairs. It irregularly published a newspaper, *Amerika's Deutsche Post*, kept vague ties with the party in the Reich, set up Nazi cells in a few American cities, and sent small contributions to Hitler. Although Teutonia never prospered, counting less than one hundred members in 1932, a few individuals within its ranks figured prominently in the subsequent history of

American Nazism: Fritz Gissibl, Walter Kappe, Sepp Schuster, and Heinz Spanknoebel.[2]

Fritz Gissibl, the founder of Teutonia, directed the Friends of the New Germany for a brief period and returned to Germany in the mid-1930's, to become associated with the Deutsches Ausland-Institut (DAI), an organization concerned with Germans living abroad. Entering the United States in 1924, the ambitious Walter Kappe joined Teutonia and later edited the newspapers of the Friends of the New Germany and the German-American Bund. He left the United States for Germany in 1937 and took a position with the DAI. During World War II Kappe helped to plan a dramatic but unsuccessful sabotage plot against the United States. Sepp Schuster entered the Nazi fold prior to the Munich Putsch, an event in which he participated. He became attached to Gissibl's organization and was active in the Friends of the New Germany. He returned to Germany in the mid-1930's and, with Gissibl, created Kameradschaft USA, a society of former Bund members. Heinz Spanknoebel remained in the United States only a few years. While a Ford Motor Company employee, he launched the Detroit wing of Teutonia. In 1933 he was most instrumental in creating the Friends of the New Germany, but in the same year difficulties with American authorities forced him to depart for the Reich.[3] Such men typified the individuals attracted to this movement: young, arrogant, resolute, fanatics firmly committed to promoting National Socialism in America.

The early 1930's saw a proliferation of small Nazi groups in the United States; their energies were focused on mobilizing disaffected German-Americans and German citizens living in America. In addition to Teutonia, the Swastika League, the Friends of the Hitler Movement, the Friends of Germany, and a few cells of the NSDAP operated out of large cities where concentrations of German-Americans lived. Usually their memberships overlapped, and each one sought to dominate the American Nazi movement.[4]

Hitler's advent to power in 1933 radically changed the fortunes of American National Socialism. Excited and encouraged by this victory, many individuals and organizations in the Third Reich were eager to carry Nazism out of the Fatherland to Germans living abroad. This interest was shared to an extent by Hitler, but in *Mein Kampf* he expressed apprehension about the effects of emigration on Germany. He disapproved of the diffusion of Germans throughout the world, believing that they would lose their racial identity by becoming mongrelized and assimilated into non-German cultures and races. According to him, the Weimar Republic had shamefully ignored this problem. A National Socialist state, on the other hand, would give Germany a new unity and inspire Germans everywhere with a sense of their uniquely historic racial mission—to dominate and carry culture to other peoples.[5] But Hitler was a continental statesman, and his chief interest in Germans outside the Reich converged on places close to Germany, notably Austria and the Sudetenland of Czechoslovakia, the two areas to which he aggressively exported Nazism and which he later integrated into Germany under the banner of national self-determination. The National Socialist movement among Germans in the United States was not one of his major concerns. In part this lack of interest reflected his inadequate knowledge of America and the German-American community.

Indeed, Hitler's view of the United States was shockingly superficial and impressionistic. Before he became chancellor, he expressed some admiration for American economic capability, especially in mass-production techniques, and considerable apprehension over the potential of American power. America's restrictive immigration laws of the 1920's helped to confirm his belief that the United States stood as a great Nordic nation, composed of the best strains of European racial stock and therefore capable of challenging German supremacy over the world. After Germany established hegemony over Europe, this threat was to be eliminated in a war with the United States. Curiously, after Hitler gained power in the 1930's this view completely changed. The inability of the United States to move swiftly out of the Depression led him to the conclusion that America was caught in an economic morass from which she would never recover. The deplorable conditions depicted in *The Grapes of Wrath,* a movie he saw several times, became for him the unchanging reality of American life. Now America simply did not count; it was a weak-willed, racially degenerate country, standing on the periphery of world affairs. America was written off in a barrage of anti-Semitic invectives. The decline of the United States had begun, Hitler believed, when the wrong side had won the Civil War, and the country's drift toward oblivion would be checked only by a revival of its German element. But other than making vague statements about German-Americans recognizing their destiny, he never specified how this rejuvenation was to be achieved.⁶ His interviews with numerous German-Americans, including Fritz Kuhn, leader of the German-American Bund, gave no further clues. After a short exchange of pleasantries, he curtly dismissed Kuhn with an ambiguous, "Go back and continue your fight." Early in his regime, in June 1933, at about the time the Friends of the New Germany was being organized, Hitler spoke in dramatic terms of the need to liberate the United States by means of an SA (Sturmabteilung) in German America.⁷

Certainly the Führer did little to thwart National Socialism in the United States, but in the mid-and late-1930's, as American Nazism reached its climax, he was too busy formulating plans for aggression on the Continent to become preoccupied with America, a country which did not enter into these calculations.

Hitler's general indifference to the United States had no effect on others in the Third Reich, who saw in German America a thrilling possibility: the creation of a powerful movement capable of fostering the aims of National Socialism. Among the impressive array of organizations committed to this task, three played an especially aggressive role: the Volksbund für das Deutschtum im Ausland (VDA), the Deutsches Ausland-Institut, and the Auslands-organisation of the NSDAP (AO). In effect, these organizations formed a Nazi International comparable to the Communist International.

The VDA, a private agency established in 1880, easily blended into Hitler's movement. For decades it had helped cement the bonds between the Fatherland and Germans overseas by promoting racial ideals through such propaganda vehicles as textbooks, calendars, and periodicals. It published world maps illustrating concentrations of Germans living abroad, and the largest element was shown residing in the United States. The VDA annually sent to thousands of German-American families a special blue candle, burned at Christmas time to symbolize ties with the Homeland and Germans throughout the world. The German-American Bund actively engaged in the sale of VDA candles. In 1938 several members of the Bund's Youth Division attended a VDA school in Germany.

Founded in 1917, the DAI adapted itself to Nazism, often collaborated with the VDA, and became the most important private organization concerned with the advancement of German racial unity. Its headquarters in Stuttgart housed a special museum and cultural center devoted to the activities of German migrants. Like the VDA, the DAI distributed propaganda materials and, more importantly, kept extensive files on Germans abroad, making this vast source of information available to any interested party in the Third Reich. The DAI loomed large in the story of American Nazism. The German-American Bund, for example, published articles in its newspaper, *Deutscher Weckruf und Beobachter,* about DAI activities and the duties of overseas Germans to the Fatherland. Numerous Bundists visited DAI headquarters in Stuttgart, and many who returned to Germany in the mid-1930's secured positions with this agency. They helped solidify a link between American Nazism and National Socialist Germany.

Of all the agencies concerned with tightening a grip on Germans everywhere, the AO was the most zealous and controversial. This branch of the Nazi party, which worked closely with the DAI and VDA, held that a German was a German only if he accepted National Socialism. Officially the AO's concern focused on German citizens in foreign countries, commonly called Reichsdeutsche. In practice it broadened this classification to include anyone of German origin by using such ambiguous terms as Volksgenosse (racial comrade), Auslandsdeutsche (German abroad), Volksdeutsche (racial German), Auslandsdeutschtum (Germandom abroad), and Grosse Deutsche Volksgemeinschaft (great German racial community). The AO always belligerently defended American Nazi groups against hostile criticism. While propagating National Socialist doctrines among German-Americans, it ran into numerous difficulties. The German Foreign Ministry frowned on its activities, and its employment of Nazi agents in America brought sharp reactions from the United States State Department. Such encumbrances diminished the AO's effectiveness, and by the late 1930's its influence in the United States became inconsequential.

This pattern of involvement in German America, ranging from a blatant exportation of Nazism in the early years of the Third Reich to a forced restraint by the late 1930's, was repeated by other propaganda agencies. Some—such as the Propaganda Ministry, headed by Joseph Goebbels, the party offices of Amt Auslandspresse, and the Volksdeutsche Mittelstelle (VoMi)—were official; others—such as the Fichtebund, Welt-Dienst (World Service), and the press agencies of the Deutsches Nachrichtenbüro (DNB) and Transozean (TO)—

were unofficial. The Fichtebund and World Service moved beyond the German-American community to reach native American fascist groups. By the mid-1930's over seventy official and unofficial organizations devoted to some aspect of Auslandsdeutschtum existed in the Third Reich. Although the functions of many overlapped or had no significance, the total effort of these agencies to influence Germans residing abroad was impressive.[8]

The direct relationship between this formidable Nazi propaganda apparatus and National Socialism in the United States can be readily illustrated in the pages of the newspapers of the Friends of New Germany and the German-American Bund. These publications made no effort to disguise their sources of information. Almost every issue contained articles from agencies in the Third Reich, clearly identifying the organization from which they originated. Reprints from the official Nazi Party paper in Germany, *Völkischer Beobachter*, often filled the pages of the *Weckruf.*

One other vital source of influence on American Nazism was Joseph Goebbels, the leading propagandist of the Third Reich. Like Hitler, he devoted most of his efforts to German and European affairs, but in the early months of the Nazi regime, before he had even consolidated his authority over a vast propaganda bureaucracy, Goebbels issued an important general directive on German propaganda in the Western hemisphere. While recognizing the prevalence of anti-German sentiment in the Americas, Goebbels believed that public opinion was fluid and capable of being manipulated to serve the interests of German foreign policy. His directive outlined the means for attaining this aim: the exploitation of German tourist and cultural agencies as well as German shipping lines and German-language newspapers; radio broadcasts and news releases from the Reich; contacts with correspondents sympathetic to National Socialist Germany; and the distribution of Nazi movies, journals, and magazines. Above all, Germany was to be pictured as a peaceful nation, struggling to free herself from an immoral and unjust Versailles Treaty; her opponents were to be seen as warmongers bent on humiliating the Reich. Goebbels saw many factors that favored German propagandists in the United States. A residue of guilt existed among influential Americans over the disparity between the idealism of Woodrow Wilson's Fourteen Points and the harsh realism of the Versailles Treaty. Bitter over the failure of Allied governments to honor their war debts to the United States, the public expressed isolationist sentiments favoring noninvolvement in European affairs. The strong Germanic influence on American culture could be exploited to develop sympathy for Germany.[9] The Propaganda Minister's instructions amounted to a detailed plan of subversion aimed at crystalizing opinion in favor of the Reich.

Goebbel's directive, coupled with the activities of the Nazi propaganda agencies, particularly the DAI and the AO, indicate the two key aims of National Socialist propaganda in America: to establish an effective power base by nazifying the German-American community and to sway American public opinion in a pro-German direction in order to prevent the United States government from offering significant opposition to Nazi policies. These aims became the central goals of the two American organizations through which much of Nazi propaganda was transmitted: the Friends of the New Germany and the German-American Bund.

In July 1933, a few months after Hitler captured power, Heinz Spanknoebel, under the authority of prominent Nazi leaders, notably Rudolf Hess and Robert Ley, created the Friends of the New Germany (Bund der Freunde des neuen Deutschlands). Assured of adequate support from Germany, Spanknoebel publicly announced his organization's connection with Reich agencies and established a weekly newspaper, *Das Neue Deutschland*, which propagated Nazi ideals.[10] He carried the title "Führer of the Nazi Party in the United States," and his first efforts concentrated on bringing together dissident pro-Nazi elements in the German-American community. Directly owing to his activities, however, both he and the Friends received some unwelcome blows. The American Führer's arrogant attempts at spreading National Socialism among German-Americans in New York City aroused a storm of public protest. A rash of violent incidents involving the Friends alerted the German and American governments. Berlin authorities, convinced that Spanknoebel's persistent movements threatened German interests, terminated his assignment. In October 1933 he left the country while under a federal grand-jury indictment for failing to register as an agent of a foreign government.

Now began an intense power struggle to fill the vacuum produced by his departure. Spanknoebel's successor was Fritz Gissibl, who was in turn followed by Reinhold Walter and later Hubert Schnuch.

Gissibl was a German national who exerted a powerful influence on the movement even after he lost the top leadership position. Walter and Schnuch were naturalized American citizens. Schnuch had been in the United States since 1913 and held impressive academic credentials, including a Ph.D. from Yale University. No important policy differences separated these men, but personal rivalries among them dissipated their energies and tore the Friends apart. No individual proved capable of commanding the loyalty and respect of the rank-and-file members. Even the establishment of the Nazi court, USCHLA (Untersuchungs-und Schlichtungs-Ausschuss, Investigation and Arbitration Committee), which existed to maintain party discipline, failed to control dissident factions. One embarrassing incident revealed the petty intrigue and disloyalty endemic within the organization. Anton Haegel, head of the New York Friends, staged a revolt against the national leadership, captured the organization's newspaper, and created a short-lived rival group called the American National Labor Party. The partisans of Haegel issued vicious verbal slurs at their opponents, broke up their meetings, and occasionally fought them in open brawls.[11]

While internal disputes worked havoc in the organization, the fiery reaction of American anti-Nazis to Hitler and National Socialism posed a threat to the Friends' future. An extremely articulate segment of the American public, composed largely of members from labor and the Jewish community, saw the Third Reich as a monstrous evil. Their concern over Hitler's abuse of Jews and his destruction of German trade unions was translated into direct action. In 1933 the American Jewish Congress organized a boycott of German goods; in March 1934 the AF of L held a mock trial of Hitler in Madison Square Garden. The apprehension of many that National Socialism would take root in America found expression in numerous publications which spotlighted the Friends' and Spanknoebel's activities.[12] The most dramatic display of interest came in early 1934 with the creation of the McCormick-Dickstein Committee to investigate Nazi activities in the United States. Samuel Dickstein, a New York congressman, was the moving force behind this special House of Representatives committee, and throughout the 1930's he played an important role in combating American Nazism. Findings of the committee received newspaper publicity and not only exposed the Nazi character of the Friends, but also pointed to its connections with American fascist organizations, such as William D. Pelley's Silver Shirts. Other testimony showed the wide ramifications of Nazi propaganda efforts, ranging from the employment of public-relations experts to the blatant use of German consulates as centers of propaganda direction. The State Department took advantage of the findings to issue protests to the Wilhelmstrasse.[13]

In response to these and other protests, German authorities reluctantly beat a strategic retreat. The Foreign Ministry sought to diminish the intensity of anti-Nazi outbursts in America, but even the AO, while defending the Friends, urged restraint on German support to American National Socialism. Several conferences between party and government officials resulted in the recall of offending consular officers, a decline in the propaganda campaign, and the severance of some of the obvious ties of the Friends to the Reich. The most difficult problem dealt with the position of German nationals active in American Nazism. In 1935, 60 percent of the 10,000 members of the Friends were Reich citizens. If this large element were to withdraw, the movement would fall apart. Fritz Gissibl argued this point to Berlin authorities to no avail; the importance of modifying anti-German sentiment in the United States remained paramount, and in late December 1935 Rudolf Hess released to the Associated Press a directive ordering all German nationals out of the Friends of the New Germany. In effect, Hess' directive divorced the Reich from the movement and completed the demise of the faction-ridden organization. The ranks of American National Socialism were severely depleted when Reich citizens withdrew and many officials and members returned to Germany.[14]

The Friends of the New Germany had a threefold significance. Its activities alarmed the American public and the government, who were concerned about the influence of a foreign-inspired organization working openly for the interests of Nazi Germany. This fact incensed Americans who harbored a profound distaste for National Socialism and served as a major irritant to German-American diplomatic relations. Moreover, the Friends failed to attract massive support from German-Americans. Through this organization the Nazi propaganda agencies beamed a campaign in anticipation of winning thousands of German-Americans to National Socialism. The German agencies held an illusion of an expanding German America and misperceived the boisterous activities of American Nazis as evidence of strength and influence. Many in Berlin saw German-Americans as the objects of a sort of irredentist effort. In fact, however, German culture in the United States had been gradually eroded away. Aside from the extreme anti-German hysteria of the World War I period, German-Americans were accepted, respected citizens and easily assimilated into American life. By the 1930's German migration to the United States had sharply diminished; many German societies had died; German-language newspapers and periodicals had decreased; and the number of German-American families with at least one member born in the Fatherland had dwindled.[15] The Nazi effort to subvert German America came at a time when this ethnic group was losing most of its emotional and other ties with Germany.

The connection between the Friends and its successor, the German-American Bund, also proved significant for the future of American National Socialism. The German-American Bund—the largest, most influential and outspoken Nazi organization ever to exist in the United States—did not suddenly appear in a vacuum; rather, it inherited the properties, organizational network, some of the members, and the troubles of the Friends of the New Germany. The framework around which the Friends had operated gave the Bund a springboard for launching a new campaign of American Nazism.

In the months immediately following Hess' directive of December 1935, Nazism in America floundered. The breakup of the Friends proceeded at a rapid pace. In order to avoid further unfavorable publicity, the party ordered Fritz Gissibl and other leaders back to Germany. The removal of the majority of Reich citizens deprived the movement of over half its membership. This was a transitional period of reorganization, when the leadership and membership composition of American National Socialism changed to predominantly American citizens of German extraction. Before he returned home in early 1936, Gissibl issued a statement to the membership lamenting the disappointments of the past year and calling for patience, unity, and self-sacrifice. More important, he named Fritz Kuhn to the leadership of American Nazism. Kuhn's background typified the new leadership of the movement. Born in Munich, Germany, in 1895, Fritz Julius Kuhn served in the German Army during World War I and participated in the Freikorps and Nazi Party activities between 1919 and 1921. He studied chemistry at the University of Munich. In 1923 he left Germany for Mexico, where he worked as an industrial chemist until 1927, when he accepted a position at the Ford Hospital laboratory in Detroit. Having joined the Friends in 1933, he rose rapidly in the movement from head of its Detroit local to leader of the midwestern units. In 1934 Kuhn became an American citizen.[16] Many leaders under Kuhn shared a similar life history: engagement in rightist activities in Germany followed by migration to America and subsequent involvement in German-American communities to further the Nazi cause.

Fritz Kuhn quickly restored vigor to the movement. At a convention in Buffalo, New York, in March 1936 the new American Führer brought numerous splinter groups and the remnants of the Friends of the New Germany into an organization which he named the Amerika-Deutscher Volksbund, or German-American Bund. Its leaders anticipated that the new title, signifying an effort at making the movement appear more American than German, would help fend off public criticism and attract native Americans to the organization. Kuhn publicly stated that the name represented the Bund's devotion to promoting friendship between Germany and the United States.[17] Later he demonstrated that the advancement of Nazism, rather than the improvement of German-American relations, was his major goal.

NOTES

1. Ludecke, *I Knew Hitler*, pp. 180-222; Hanighen, "Foreign Political Movements in the United States," p. 5.
2. Frye, *Nazi Germany and the American Hemisphere, 1933-1941*, pp. 32-33; Arthur Smith, *The Deutschtum of Nazi Germany and the United States*, pp. 61-62; Strong, *Organized Anti-Semitism in America*, p. 21.
3. Arthur Smith, pp. 62-63.
4. U.S., Dept. of Justice, *German-American Bund. Outline of Evidence*, pp. 6-7 (hereafter cited as *Bund*); Hawgood, *The Tragedy of German America*, pp. 303-304; Strong, pp. 21-22; Arthur Smith, pp. 66-71. An excellent study of pre-1933 American Nazism is Diamond, "The Years of Waiting: National Socialism in the United States, 1922-1933."
5. Hitler, *Mein Kampf*, pp. 394-398.
6. Compton, *The Swastika and the Eagle*, pp. 3-38; Weinberg, "Hitler's Image of the United States."
7. Compton, p. 15; Rogge, *The Official German Report*, p. 119; Rauschning, *The Voice of Destruction*, p. 68.

8. For a more detailed analysis of Nazi propaganda agencies, see Zeman, *Nazi Propaganda,* pp. 38-75; Murphy, *et al, National Socialism*, pp. 93-130.
9. Kris, "German Propaganda Instructions of 1933."
10. Because of inadequate finances and internal troubles, the newspaper of the Friends of the New Germany frequently changed titles. In succession the Friends published *Das Neue Deutschland, Die Deutsche Zeitung, Deutscher Beobachter*, and the *Weckruf.*
11. *Deutscher Weckruf und Beobachter*, October 17, 1935; June 13, 1936 (cited hereafter as *Weckruf*); Arthur Smith, pp. 71-80; Hare, *The Brown Network* pp. 239-262; Hawgood, pp. 304-305; Strong, pp. 23-24. Designed to conceal internal discord from the public, USCHLA was used by the Friends and modeled after the court of the NSDAP. Little is known of its secret activities in America, but it was obviously ineffective in preserving the authority of the Friends' leadership. It did not function under the Bund.
12. Lore, "Nazi Politics in America"; Tigner, "Will America Go Fascist?"; Morgan, "Swastika"; Winner, "Fascism at the Door." These give only a small sampling of the flood of anti-Nazi articles appearing in American journals throughout the 1930's.
13. U.S., Congress, House, Special Committee on Un-American Activities, *Investigation of Nazi and other Propaganda*; Arthur Smith, pp. 81-82; DeJong, *The German Fifth Column in the Second World War*, pp. 23-24.
14. Frye, pp. 57-64; Arthur Smith, pp. 83-85; New York *Times*, December 25, 1935 (hereafter cited as *Times*).
15. Remak, "Friends of the New Germany: the Bund and German-American Relations," p. 41; Bischoff, *Nazi Conquest Through German Culture*, pp. 167-169; Wittke, *The German Language Press in America* pp. 262-263; Hawgood, pp. 287-303.
16. Arthur Smith, p. 91; Strong, pp. 24-26; Frye, p. 80; *Weckruf*, September 26; December 30, 1935.
17. *Times*, April 1, 1936; *Bund*, pp. 9-10; *Weckruf*, April 2, 16; June 13, 1936.

2
THE ANATOMY OF
A HATE MOVEMENT

The years 1936 and 1937 brought a marked increase in the fortunes of American National Socialism. Fritz Kuhn molded the German-American Bund into an aggressive organization, far surpassing the Friends of the New Germany in dedication and militancy. Bundists dramatically characterized their movement as Kämpfendes Deutschtum (fighting Germandom) and exposed all its Nazi trappings to the public.

As in the Third Reich, the Führerprinzip (leadership principle) formed the basic organizational pattern of the German-American Bund. Bundesführer Kuhn stood at the top of the organization's hierarchy, and the leadership principle gave him absolute authority in every sphere of Bund affairs. He could mediate grievances, appoint or remove officers, revoke the membership of any Bundist at any time, convene an annual national convention, and interpret Bund regulations. Kuhn had full power of ownership over Bund property, including funds, equipment, buildings, and land holdings. He controlled all the Bund's subsidiary organizations. He could fix dues and other financial assessments as well as organize, enlarge, divide, or disband units. His authority was limited only by the national convention, which could reelect or depose him. Beneath the Bundesführer the organization broadened out in typical pyramidal fashion: a small group of national officers, including a secretary, press agent, public-relations director, treasurer, and deputy Führer; officials of the subsidiary organizations—camps, DKV (Deutscher Konsum Verband, the Bund's economic corporation), women's and youth divisions; regional, county, and city Führers; and finally the rank-and-file members. Each leader or Führer recognized the authority of his immediate superior, and all viewed their prime loyalty to the Bund as personified in the Bundesführer.[1] During Kuhn's tenure of office, this organizational framework worked well and helped to check the problem of internal dissension which had plagued the Friends of the New Germany. All Bund members were required to pledge their acceptance of the Führerprinzip, and the Bundesführer repeatedly emphasized its importance as the mainstay of the movement's internal solidarity.

The Bund inherited from the Friends of the New Germany an organization divided into three regions or Gaue: east, midwest, and west. "Gau," an obsolete German word with racial overtones, was revived by the Nazis and may be loosely translated as "subdivision of the tribe." National Bund headquarters were located at 178 East Eighty-fifth Street in the heart of New York City's German-American community of Yorkville. The eastern Gau worked out of this office, the midwest Gau operated from Chicago, the western one from Los Angeles. Each Gau was broken into divisions corresponding to American states. Further subdivisions carried the organization down to the local group, or Ortsgruppe. The most typical unit was on the city level. Each regional leader, or Gauleiter, directed the local units in his area and had a staff similar to the Bundesführer's. Although the Bund claimed members in every state except Louisiana, its own listings of locals reveal that the organization operated chiefly out of northern and eastern urban areas. Locals of the eastern region included Albany, Astoria, the Bronx, Brooklyn, Buffalo, Glendale, Jamaica, Lindenhurst, Nassau County, New Rochelle, Manhattan, Poughkeepsie, Rochester, Rockland County, Schenectady, South Brooklyn, Staten Island, Syracuse, Troy, Utica, White Plains, and Yonkers in New York; Baltimore, Maryland; Washington, D.C.; Bergen County, Hudson County, Newark, Passaic County, and Trenton in New Jersey; Boston, Massachusetts; Bridgeport, Danbury, Greenwich, New Britain, New Haven, Norwalk, Stamford, and Waterbury in Connecticut; Providence, Rhode Island; and Lancaster, Philadelphia, Pittsburgh, Reading, and Sellersville in Pennsylvania. Locals of the midwest region embraced Chicago and South Chicago, Illinois; Cincinnati, Cleveland, Dayton, and Toledo in Ohio; Detroit, Michigan; Fort Wayne, Gary, Hammond, Indianapolis, and South Bend in Indiana; Kenosha, Milwaukee, and Sheboygan, in Wisconsin; Minneapolis and St. Paul, Minnesota; Omaha, Nebraska; St. Louis, Missouri; and Taylor, Texas. Locals of the western region included Los Angeles, Oakland, Concord, Petaluma, Santa Barbara, San Diego, San Francisco, and San Gabriel in California; Salt Lake City, Utah; Portland, Oregon; and Seattle and Spokane in Washington.[2] This listing shows the nationwide network of the movement; its center of strength, however, came from the New York metropolitan area. In this locality, where the largest number of German-Americans lived, the Bund staged its most dramatic activities and found its greatest concentration of support.

Among the individuals attracted to the Bund were recently naturalized German-American citizens and native Americans as well as German nationals. Some members were alienated misfits, others, such as Fritz Kuhn, had the persistence of fanatics. But most saw the Bund as a social outlet and sincerely believed that it represented a patriotic American organization. Very little information is available on the socioeconomic status of the average member. Apparently few individuals of professional rank, wealth, and education joined the Bund; the available specific evidence indicates that it was an urban lower-middle-class movement.[3]

The presence of German nationals in the Bund perplexed and troubled its critics. Some of them charged that the majority of Bund members were un-American aliens. Though this accusation was not true, Kuhn had disregarded Hess' directive of December 1935 by creating an affiliated group known as the Prospective Citizens League, or the Citizens Protective League, which admitted German nationals into the Bund. The League preferred to accept only those Germans who had taken out their first papers toward American citizenship. Kuhn restricted their activities by ordering them to remain aloof from politics and excluding them from leadership positions in the Bund. Thus German nationals did attain full membership status; anyone could become a Bund member provided he accepted the leadership principle and was of Aryan stock free of Black or Jewish blood.[4] The fact that the Bund never released its actual number of members led to wild speculations about its numerical strength. Estimates of membership varied with the sympathy of the observer. Fritz Kuhn always inflated the number; newspaper and magazine articles presented greatly exaggerated figures, ranging from 50,000 to 500,000. According to the Department of Justice, at the height of its power, in 1937 and 1938, the Bund had approximately 8,500 members and 5,000 or 6,000 anonymous sympathizers. Aliens comprised about 25 percent of this total; the majority were naturalized Americans who had fought for Germany in World War I and had migrated to America in the immediate postwar years.[5]

A division of the German-American Bund known as the Ordnungsdienst (Order Service), or OD, was a paramilitary unit patterned after the SA. Carried over from the Friends of the New Germany, it gained a high level of discipline under the Bund, having among its members the most dedicated and fanatical Bundists. Fully outfitted in fascist uniforms including a Sam Brown belt and swastika arm band, OD men engaged in military drill exercises and rifle practice. They marched and paraded at Bund gatherings, where they acted as guards and flag bearers and were treated as an elite group. Since future leaders of the movement were to be drawn from the Order Service, each OD man underwent rigorous training. His personal life came second to his obligations and sacrifices to the Bund. Even at the risk of his life he was expected to defend the Bund against internal and external attacks and to commit himself entirely to National Socialist philosophy. Twice a week he attended meetings where he practiced German military formations, learned the principles of National Socialism, and was trained in jujitsu. At the close of the gatherings the group sang the "Horst Wessel Song" and the "Battle Song of the SA" which every OD man had memorized. Smoking and drinking were forbidden, and an unexcused absence from an OD meeting was followed by strict punishment.[6] The Bund slogan of Kämpfendes Deutschtum found concrete expression in this private police force composed of specially trained loyal and obedient fighters ready to make every effort and risk everything to advance the movement.

Apart from the OD, the Bund waged a vigorous campaign to win support from German-American youth. The leaders assumed that their organization was destined to exist in America indefinitely, and they perceived that new recruits could not come from Germany. The future of the organization depended on its ability to win young adherents from the German community in the United States. To capture this youth, the Bund devoted considerable time and organization. Its ultimate goal was to bring the entire German-American youth into the Youth Division of the Bund.

The Bund always characterized its youth in romantic yet awesome terms, similar to Hitler's descriptions of the ideal German youth. Youth Division Director Theodore Dinkelacker wrote of a dedicated, proud youth, eager for combat and sacrifice to further the goals of American National Socialism. When facing the reality of capturing new youth members, however, he recognized that a key factor lay in preventing German assimilation into American culture. He charged that the anti-German propaganda of World War I had caused the loss of German-American identity. German-American children reared in the war environment experienced humiliations and came to doubt and suspect the Homeland. They grew to distrust their parents and accepted as fact the propaganda that Germans were Huns who had crucified Canadian soldiers and cut off the hands of Belgian babies. This kind of influence had estranged German-American children from their parents. In order for young people to recapture the heritage of the German race, the Bund urged parents to bring their children into the Youth Division.[7]

Modeled after the Hitler Youth, the Youth Division displayed the features of Nazism, and political indoctrination formed an essential part of the training. At Saturday evening meetings members took lessons in German, received instructions on how to salute the swastika, and learned to sing the "Horst Wessel Song" and other Nazi favorites. They became familiar with the life stories of Nazi heroes and listened to Hitler's speeches on shortwave radio. They were encouraged to correspond with Hitler Youth members in Germany. Their uniforms resembled those worn by youth in the Third Reich, complete with swastika buckles and a lightening-bolt insignia which symbolized the power of Nordic youth to overcome all evil. During parades at the camps, boys often carried the short dagger at the hip inscribed with "Blut und Ehre" (blood and honor).[8] The intensity of the indoctrination program is reflected in an essay written by a seventeen-year-old girl. She expressed concern over the Jews' alleged persecution of Germans in the United States, and in simplistic terms she presented the usual Nazi and Bund propaganda: while Germany slept during the Weimar years, Jews captured control of all the professions and political offices; the same situation was currently developing in the United States. She called for an awakened German-American community, under Bund leadership, to arouse America in time to prevent a Jewish take-over.[9] Such ludicrous remarks cannot be dismissed lightly, for they show the passion of one true believer, which was shared by many individuals in the movement.

The main source of indoctrination was the Youth Division's monthly magazine, *Junges Volk*, appearing irregularly between January 1937 and December 1940. This magazine carried photographs of Bund gatherings, correspondence between members and youth in Germany, and essays on teen-age hobbies and sports. Fiction and editorials in *Junges Volk* stressed several themes.[10] One was the moral uplift German-American youth experienced by joining Bund youth groups. Without proper supervision, the editors warned, German-American children drifted into pool halls, learned bad language, came into contact with obscene literature, saw evil movies, and at an early age learned to smoke cigarettes and drink alcoholic beverages. Like many American teen-agers influenced by a bad environment, they developed into juvenile delinquents. They forgot that German blood flowed in their veins, and they lost respect for the language, customs, and traditions of the Fatherland. Once German-American teen-agers became part of the Bund youth, however, they regained respect for German culture, preferred healthy hikes to immoral movies, and engaged in constructive activities in an atmosphere of racial comradeship.

Tribute was paid to German-American contributions to American history. The role of Germans in the American Revolution—particularly of Peter Muhlenberg, Nicholas Herkimer, and Baron von Steuben —received special attention, with the clear implication that the Germans, more than any other ethnic group, pushed the Colonies toward independence and later became the staunchest defenders of the new American nation. With such a magnificent tradition behind them, German-American children should not be ashamed of their ancestry. Indeed, they must treasure this heritage. And inevitably, the dialogue drifted back to the need for America to preserve a Nordic-Germanic racial makeup. American youth of German descent might look at the polyglot nature of American society and wonder who really represented the United States. Orientals, Blacks, southern and eastern Europeans, and Jews filled the streets of the nation's cities. This mixture of races obscured the fact that Germans had settled the land long before these "swarms of human parasites" had arrived on American shores. A German youth determined to uphold racial identity could help America regain her true race consciousness. Here in capsule form is a belief Bundists constantly instilled in their youth: Germans held a uniquely powerful, if not dominant, position in shaping the course of American history, and only by maintaining this strong German influence could America attain greatness.

Nazified German history filled many of the pages of *Junges Volk*. The typical account related centuries of German disunity and ended happily with a tremendous upsurge of national fusion under the Hitler movement. Since ancient times Germany had remained a divided land, where blood brothers fought against each other in petty, unnecessary wars. The ravages of Roman legions, Charlemagne's invasions, and the marauding armies of the Thirty Years War had dismembered Germany. The Germans in Napoleon's armies forgot their own land and people and died on the steppes of Russia for an alien cause. In the World War Germans again faced Germans in an orgy of self-destruction. Finally, after the war, hope came from a common soldier, a man who called for a strong, great, united Germany free of foreign controls and influences. Adolf Hitler's leadership and message inspired Germans everywhere with pride and a new sense of awareness in being German. The youth of German America were alert to his call and, while remaining good Americans, would join his struggle to unify Germans throughout the world.

Curious comparisons between American and Nazi heroes were brought to the attention of the young readers. Abraham Lincoln and Horst Wessel were viewed as typical figures of the time in which they lived and died. The martyred President had fought against national disunity, while Horst Wessel died in an attempt to keep Germany from plunging into a bitter civil war and becoming the bastion of world revolution. The cowardly assassination of both heroes prevented them from seeing the fulfillment of their life's work. Yet after death their dreams became reality: black slaves gained freedom, and Germany under the Third Reich freed herself from the slavery of Jewish Bolshevism. Young German-Americans held both men in reverence.

Anti-Semitic fiction covered the pages of the magazine. One story reported how the youth of Russia had been systematically eliminated by Jews who sat in the Kremlin and signed orders for arrest and imprisonment. Another told of a boy and a girl who attended a school where most students came from Jewish families; like the students, the teachers had Communist sympathies and taught only anti-German and antifascist hate propaganda; the two German children did their best to foil this indoctrination. Poetry conveyed the warning of a Jewish revolutionary plot to destroy American institutions. Editorials supplemented fictional accounts of alleged Jewish perfidy. Jews worked in numerous ways to create a Soviet America; they masqueraded as pacifists, liberals, and democrats and lectured in schools and colleges on the virtues of Communism. On May Day Jews crowded the streets to demonstrate their sympathy for Communist terror. American patriots were urged to change this course set by a racially alien people, to eradicate the cancer of Jewish Communism from American life. Force might become necessary to save America. If so, German-American youth would be in the front ranks fighting this evil foe.

Junges Volk editors candidly admitted that the Hitler Youth in Germany provided inspiration for the Bund Youth in America. After observing the German youth movement with its magnificent parades and excellent training organizations, the editors expressed regret at seeing American young people gathering in cellars, suffering from inadequate facilities, and facing hostility from large numbers of Americans. But far from losing heart, youth leaders assured their followers that outward appearances meant little when compared to the inner meaning and spiritual strength of the Bund Youth. Although it would probably never match the numerical size of the Hitler Youth, the Youth Division of the Bund could and did equal the quality of youth in Germany. In comradeship, willingness to sacrifice, discipline, and ability at sports and games, it could easily be pitted against any other German group in the world. The Jewish, Communist, and Black influences thrust upon them in American schools only tested and reinforced their courage and strength. Ultimately they would prevail and win the struggle, for like Germans everywhere, they possessed a unique and fighting determination to win.

The Bund Youth Division was usually subdivided into two age groupings for each sex: eight to thirteen and fourteen to eighteen. At eighteen boys might become youth leaders or enter the OD; girls were encouraged to join the Women's Auxiliary. Bund women generously offered their services, especially at camps and to youth groups, training girls in homemaking. In 1937 local units having youth groups in the eastern Gau were Hudson County and Newark, New Jersey; Astoria, the Bronx, Brooklyn, Buffalo, Jamaica, Manhattan, Nassau County, Schenectady, South Brooklyn, Westchester County, and Yonkers, New York; and Philadelphia, Pennsylvania. Youth groups in the midwest Gau included Detroit, Michigan; Chicago, Illinois; and Milwaukee, Wisconsin; and in the western Gau, Los Angeles, California.[11]

Sensational displays of Nazism occurred at the various Bund Camps. The Deutschhorst Country Club near Croyden, Pennsylvania; Camp Hindenburg near Grafton, Wisconsin; Effende Camp near Detroit, Michigan; and Camp Sutter near Los Angeles, California, all had modest facilities with at least one permanent building to serve as a meeting place for members on weekends as well as for youth quarters in the summer months. Other camp sites, without facilities, included areas near Buffalo and Schenectady, New York; Spokane and Seattle, Washington; Portland, Oregon; and Los Angeles, San Diego, and Oakland, California. The two largest and most important camps operated through subsidiary organizations: Camp Siegfried located at Yaphank, Long Island, functioned through the German-American Settlement League, and the German-American Auxiliary held the title to Camp Nordland at Andover, New Jersey. Bundesführer Fritz Kuhn headed both corporations. Siegfried and Nordland had a restaurant, a meeting hall, parade and sports grounds, streets named after Nazi leaders—Adolf Hitler and Herman Göring Streets at Camp Siegfried—swimming pools, bungalows often with swastikas embedded in the masonry, and tents or cabins for young people participating in summer programs. Siegfried was established in 1935 under the Friends of the New Germany; Nordland was founded in 1937.[12]

The Bund advertised both camps as retreats where German-Americans would find fellowship among racial companions, participate in health-restoring recreation, and enjoy good food and beverages at nominal prices. Ten cents bought admission; meals cost thirty-five cents and up; overnight accommodations were available for seventy-five cents. Distributions of mimeographed maps at Bund meetings directed members to the camps, and chartered trains and buses often carried large crowds to them for special celebrations.[13]

Recreation may have been the concern of most of the people who came, but the Bund leadership gave a higher significance to Siegfried and Nordland. Carl Nicolay, one of the movement's intellectuals, related the establishment of Camp Nordland to a compelling spiritual and racial need peculiar only to people of Nordic ancestry. He maintained that long ago, in the obscure mists of man's early history, the camp life of the Nordics originated a unique conception of a community oriented toward blood and soil. Around their campfires in the forest, near streams, on mountain tops and in valleys, the racially pure Nordics joyfully and reverently celebrated nature rites, such as the coming of seasons, and achieved a communion with God and nature which enabled them to penetrate the deepest mysteries of the universe. Their spiritual fulfillment was accompanied by rigorous physical activity, which gave the Nordics strong and beautiful bodies capable of working, hunting, and fighting to maintain their racial identity. This healthy existence met man's most complete spiritual and physical needs and found concrete expression after a hard day of work and endurance when the Nordics returned to their camps to enjoy food, wine, song, and comradeship in the warm, golden glow of the fire. Nicolay argued that Germans in America needed similar camps to give them courage and strength to fight for their racial existence and to gain solace after the daily struggle to sustain their economic livelihood. The Bund camps must become a source of rejuvenation for German-Americans, especially for young people, and not function merely as outlets for weekend excursions. At other times the Bund leadership expressed the meaning of the camps in more concrete terms. They were designated as pieces of German soil in America, where the prime goal was the inculcation of National Socialism into German-Americans. The camps were to be centers of National Socialist politics, breathing and propagating the spirit of the Third Reich. Bundists frequently referred to the camps as representing the American counterpart of Kraft durch Freude (Strength through Joy), an organization allied to the Nazi Labor Front in Germany. Like Kraft durch Freude, the camps provided the facilities for inexpensive holidays mixed with ideology.[14]

Much of the activity was directed at young people. During the summer of 1937 several hundred children camped at Siegfried and Nordland, remaining from one to eight weeks at the cost of five dollars per child each week. A typical day of training began at 6:30

A.M. when the children awoke to a bugle call. Lessons in German and the principles of National Socialism, along with swimming, hiking, and physical exercises, occupied the main part of the day's program. Before each meal groups gathered around a flagpole to salute German and American flags. At night they formed circles about campfires to listen to shortwave broadcasts from Germany, sing Hitler Youth songs, and relate the life stories of Nazi leaders.[15]

The camp facilities also provided the atmosphere for a miniature Nazi open-air rally. A typical affair occurred on May 1, 1937, when the Bund staged a celebration at Camp Nordland commemorating National Socialist May Day. Youth and OD groups played a predominant part in the proceedings. Fritz Kuhn reviewed their parade with outstretched arm, in the tradition of Hitler. Afterward he and other Bund leaders treated the crowd to harangues in which they glorified the achievements of the National Socialist economy, pointed to the dignity it gave to labor, and slashed at Communism for poisoning workers' minds by preaching class hatred and fomenting strikes. The Bundists urged American workers to join their organization because it exposed the Communist menace and fought for a harmonious cooperation between capital and labor. Between speeches the crowd watched gymnastic exercises and listened to a band play "The Star Spangled Banner" and the marches "Frederick the Great" and "Sieg Heil Kuhn." The camp buildings and parade platforms held large banners carrying the slogan "No Freedom Without a Struggle." At the end of the ceremony the crowd broke up to picnic and drink beer. OD men circulated through the gatherings, distributing and selling the Bund newspaper and propaganda leaflets.[16]

Following the example of the NSDAP, the Bund viewed the mass rally as a propaganda technique and a way of instilling a fighting élan into its members. In New York City, in 1937, the organization held three or four rallies a week at auditoriums such as the Hippodrome and Ebling's Casino, where attendance varied between fifty and five thousand people. Usually admission cost twenty-five cents to one dollar. The meetings were announced by glaring placards proclaiming: "Come to the Mass Protest Meeting Against the Unconstitutional Jewish Boycott," or, "Join the Giant Protest Demonstration against Communist-Inspired Murders." Nazi slogans hung conspicuously throughout the meeting hall: "Deutschland Erwache" (Germany Awake), "Ein Volk, Ein Reich, Ein Führer" (One Race, One Germany, One Leader), or "Wir Amerikaner Deutschen Blutes Ehren die Heimat" (We Americans of German Blood Honor the Homeland). The swastika and the American flag decorated the speakers' platform. Designed to impress members and outsiders, the rallies were noisy, belligerent, and joyous affairs, complete with marching bands, fascist salutes, stamping feet, rousing applause, thunderous "Sieg Heils," and the singing of Nazi songs. Before the speeches began, OD groups carried modified Nazi standards into the hall. They consisted of a silver eagle mounted on top of a pole, below which hung tassels and a flag inscribed with a swastika identifying the Gau of the OD unit. After the rally the crowd enjoyed refreshments and a dance or watched a Nazi film.[17]

The proceeds from the camps and rallies were a chief source of income for the Bund. The sale of the organization's newspaper, *Deutscher Weckruf und Beobachter*, provided additional funds. Published weekly, the main New York edition was supplemented by three other *Weckruf* in Philadelphia, Chicago, and Los Angeles. Each paper carried the same news and editorials, but advertisements varied with the region. An annual subscription cost three dollars, and the combined circulation reached 10,000 copies in the summer of 1938.[18] The paper varied in size from four to thirty pages, with the usual length at eight to ten pages. In the early years most of the paper was printed in German; by the fall of 1937, however, the German-language section had become smaller and the headlines, feature articles, and editorials appeared in English. This pattern remained relatively constant until late 1939, when most of the editorials and anti-Semitic articles returned to German. The paper's format followed a general design. International, national, or local events affecting the Bund appeared on the front page. An editoral page was followed by a section dealing with news of Gau affairs. The last pages contained advertisements for German beer, restaurants, pork shops, and haberdashery stores, along with filler articles acquired from American anti-Semitic sources or Nazi propaganda agencies.

Bundists called the *Weckruf* "our battle press" and claimed that, while sympathizing with Germany and National Socialism, it had no ties with the German government. In fact, however, Reich agencies in part subsidized the newspaper by advertising German tourist, railroad, and steamship companies. Until 1939 the paper received $800 a month from these sources.[19]   Bund editors pretentiously maintained that the paper's policy represented the views of nine-tenths of all German-Americans, who had no voice in the American press. The *Weckruf* displayed all the features of the worst kind of yellow journalism. Astonishingly frank and outspoken, the paper made no effort at objective news reporting. There was no politeness, no mincing of words. Bold black headlines sensationalized the news and usually carried an anti-Semitic message. Since this weekly publication magnified the growth and prestige of National Socialism, its interpretation of events conveyed the impression that the world revolved around Germany and the Bund. The editors candidly admitted that they published Nazi propaganda. Much space was given to photographic essays on Nazi meetings and demonstrations, German technical and military progress, and Hitler's varied social and political activities. Full coverage went to Nazi Party rallies and the important speeches of Hitler, Hess, and Goebbels. German-Americans and others wishing to orient themselves to National Socialism were urged to read the *Weckruf*.

Newspaper circulation drives remained a constant in the Bund's history. Members received instructions to "spread the fight through our newspaper" by winning new subscribers and advertisers. An expanded circulation helped broaden the movement's appeal and brought money needed to defray expenses. Another source of income was membership dues. After paying a three-dollar initiation fee, each member was assessed seventy-five cents a month. The organization was thus assured of a steady supply of funds, but it hardly became wealthy. In addition, the Bund received small contributions from anonymous sympathizers. The Bund's critics assumed that it drew large financial outlays from the German government, but there is little evidence that strong monetary links existed. The Bund operated largely on its own resources; it managed to break even each year until the expenses of legal battles threw its finances into chaos. Like the Nazi Party in the early 1920's, its main sources of income were proceeds from rallies and celebrations, the sale of propaganda materials, particularly the *Weckruf*, and membership dues.

The Bund's economic corporation, DKV, also called the German-American Business League, received wide publicity but gave the movement little in profits. Its origins date from the period of the Friends of the New Germany when, in reaction to the boycott of

German goods by various anti-Nazi and Jewish societies, the Friends promoted the Deutsch-Amerikanische Wirtschafts-Ausschuss (DAWA, German-American Protective Alliance). The DAWA was shortlived. It became a casualty of the break-up of the Friends but was resurrected as the DKV and actively promoted by the Bund. The main intent of the DKV was expressed in its slogans: "Patronize Gentile Stores Only," "Buy German," "Aryan Buying Pays Aryan Men," and, "Tell yourselves and your relatives and your friends, buy Aryan every day." By encouraging German-Americans and Bund members to deal exclusively with German or Aryan businesses, the DKV hoped to strike back at the anti-German boycott, to promote trade between Germany and the United States, and to increase the sale of German-made products in America. To achieve these goals, it published lists of firms sympathizing with the anti-German boycott, issued guides listing businesses affiliated with the DKV, and offered discounts and trading stamps to customers. The Bund newspaper gave extensive coverage to this agency's activities. An annual Christmas Exposition and Market held in New York took as its motto "Buy German for Christmas" and became the most important DKV event. Booths displayed German-made goods along with Bund propaganda. Representatives of the German consulate in New York and Bund officials attended opening-night exercises to deliver addresses stressing the magnificence of the exposition and its helpfulness in binding Germans, Germany, and the United States together.[20]

Promotion of DKV·affairs was always accompanied by a snipe at Samuel Untermeyer and his Non-Sectarian Anti-Nazi League, the chief sponsor of the boycott of German goods. This league took Nazism and the Bund to be serious menaces to America and urged all Americans to boycott everything German just as they would quarantine a contagious disease. Bundists caricatured Untermeyer as the Jewish general who commanded the "Non-Aryan Anti-American League to Champion Jewish Business" and claimed that his activities constituted an un-American boycott racket designed to impair the peaceful relations between Germany and the United States. Fritz Kuhn wrote to Postmaster General James A. Farley demanding government action in stopping the Non-Sectarian League from using "Hit Hitler" stickers on envelopes going through the U.S. mails. This misuse of the mails, Kuhn charged, showed how Jewish and Communist boycotters used American institutions to threaten democracy by disseminating personal grievances, hatred, and subversion. Moreover, this shameful activity insulted the large German-American element of the taxpaying public who might be encouraged to retaliate against Jewish malcontents.[21]

According to Bund writers, however, the boycott had backfired, producing results directly opposite to those anticipated. It aroused German resentment and created an anti-Semitic situation in Germany. Jewish reports on its successes were lies; in fact, tourist trade to Germany had increased and Germany had shown great ability to capture new export outlets in Europe and South America. In the end, the United States suffered more than Germany: a spiteful minority hindered American economic recovery, poisoned the atmosphere of international relations, and created domestic turmoil by illegal picketing and restraints on trade.[22] This whole attack on the Non-Sectarian Anti-Nazi League represented typical Bund thinking. All opponents were invested with the most evil characteristics, and their goals and methods were labeled undemocratic. On the other hand, the Bund pictured itself as the defender of American institutions and the champion of a persecuted German-American community.

The DKV and all the other Bund affiliates were coordinated by Fritz Kuhn. As Bundesführer he faced the formidable task of wielding these branches of the organization into an efficient, cohesive movement. His method of communication demonstrated one way of attaining this goal. He gave orders through written Commands which were to be faithfully fulfilled. Each local leader received a copy to transmit to his group. The Bundesführer held these men responsible for administering his instructions, which included reading the Commands to members at special meetings. A report was then returned to national headquarters verifying compliance with the Commands.

Throughout 1936 and early 1937 Kuhn's Commands affirmed several points. One emphasized the obligation of members to celebrate Nazi holidays as well as certain American ones. Indeed, Kuhn proclaimed two days—George Washington's birthday in February and Hitler's birthday in April—as official Bund holidays, which had to be celebrated in grand style by all units. The Washington celebration could be conducted either in English or in German and, like Hitler's birthday, was to be entirely public and under the full scrutiny of the American and German-American press. On July 4, American Independence Day, Bund units were urged to join the parades of the American Legion. Most of Kuhn's listings, however, focused on important Nazi holidays, such as November 9, commemorating the Munich Putsch; National Socialist Labor Day on May 1; the January 30 Reich Anniversary celebration; and the anniversary of the death of Horst Wessel on February 23. If possible, Bund members were to honor these affairs in conjunction with or under the direction of German consulates or other Reich representatives. Invitations were to be sent to all local non-Bund German-Americans. Following each event the unit leader was to collect local newspaper articles about it and send them to national headquarters.[23]

Kuhn was also concerned with identifying the friends and enemies of his movement. Units were kept busy gathering material written about the Bund, the German element in the United States, Germany, Jews, and Communists. Furthermore, Kuhn ordered unit leaders to keep a card file which would identify former members, active members, sympathizers, and enemies of the organization. The Bundesführer placed great importance on the file, suggesting that it could be used for punitive action: it would facilitate identification of Germans hostile to the Third Reich for German authorities. But in this early period of his leadership Kuhn's greatest interest was reserved for communication within the organization. He wanted a network so rapid and effective that it could alarm members and friends in the shortest possible time, disseminate propaganda rapidly, and make possible the calling of a mass meeting within one day.[24]

The national convention was the movement's most important unifying device. Usually located in New York, these conventions were annual assemblies attended by hundreds of Bund members. Each unit was headed by the local leader and included one delegate for every fifty members. Local units bore the costs of travel, but delegates received free accommodations upon arrival at national headquarters. Designed to solidify ranks, review policies, propose new programs, and elect a national leader, the convention helped maintain the fervor of the movement and enhance the members' morale. Important Bund leaders addressed the gathering, always predicting an optimistic future for American Nazism. Communists and Jews were assailed, and the movement's struggle against them was proclaimed in a do-or-die manner. Concurrent with meetings in New York City, more dramatic celebrations and recreational affairs occurred at Camps Siegfried and Nordland. The 1937 convention was a bellicose event in which the Bund arrogantly displayed its devotion to Nazism. At the end of the sessions Kuhn made public the contents of telegrams he had sent to Hitler and to German propaganda agencies. His communication to the German Chancellor announced the Bund's "undying union with the Homeland." The telegrams to the VDA and the AO acknowledged the Bund's common work with Germans everywhere and declared support for the fulfillment of the goals of these agencies. [25] At this time in the Bund's history Kuhn felt supremely self-confident but erroneously believed that a haughty display of Nazism would attract American support.

NOTES

1. *Constitution of the German-American Bund*, in National Archives, Record Group 131 (cited hereafter as RG 131), Box 104.
2. *Kämpfendes Deutschtum*, 1937, p. 38; 1938, p. 50. The Bund's yearbooks were published only in 1937 and 1938.
3. Strong, *Organized Anti-Semitism*, pp. 33-34. Strong investigated Bund members in the Chicago area and, on the basis of their residences, concluded that they came from lower-middle class origins.
4. Bund Command No. 3, October 30, 1936 (all Bund Commands are in RG 131, Box 16). Membership applications and cards make specific reference to the leadership principle and specify the Aryan racial requirement. RG 131, Boxes 1 and 15.
5. DeJong, *The German Fifth Column*, p. 276.
6. *The OD of the German-American Bund*, in RG 131, Box 16; *Bund*, pp. 24-32; U.S., Congress, House, Special Committee on Un-American Activities, *Investigation of Un-American Propaganda*, pp. 1443-1469, 1584-1620 (hereafter cited as *Un-American Propaganda*).
7. *Kämpfendes Deutschtum*, 1937, p. 30; *Weckruf*, February 11, September 23, 1937; *German American Youth: Here's Where You Belong*, in RG 131, Box 101. There was an element of truth in the Bund's argument. German-Americans did face harassment during the World War. Nevertheless, historically European ethnic identities generally faded away by the third generation.
8. *Bund*, pp. 33-34; *Un-American Propaganda*, pp. 1449-1459.
9. A notebook containing several essays written by Bund Youth Division members is in RG 131, Box 143.
10. *Junges Volk*, January 1937-May 1939, in RG 131, Box 104.
11. *Kämpfendes Deutschtum*, 1937, p. 42; Bund Youth Division leaflets, in RG 131, Boxes 143 and 101.
12. *Bund*, pp. 41-42; *Weckruf*, June 13, 1936.
13. *Welcome to Camp Siegfried on Long Island*, in RG 131, Box 121; *Weckruf*, July 16, 1936; August 12, September 23, 1937; "Uncle Sam's Nazis."
14. *Weckruf*, July 29, 1937; February 11, 1937; *Bund*, p. 41.

15. *Weckruf*, November 26, 1936; August 12, 1937; *Junges Volk*, Summer 1937; *Bund*, pp. 34-35.
16. *May Day Celebration in Honor of National Labor*, in RG 131, Box 140, photographs, Box 18. Propaganda leaflets from Nazi agencies came with the crews of German ships who often visited the camps while on shore leave. See *Bund*, pp. 75-76. During the summer months many of the camps' celebrations attracted more than ten thousand people. See Carlson, *Under Cover*, pp. 108-110, for a colorful account of a day at Camp Siegfried.
17. Accounts of the mass rallies fill the pages of the Bund newspaper. Bund writers always emphasized the tremendous number of people who allegedly attended them, as well as the exuberant enthusiasm displayed, implying that the movement had an almost irresistible appeal to German-Americans and to other Americans who were waking up to the dangers of Jewish Bolshevism. For an excellent account of a rally, see *Weckruf*, February 18, 1937. This report is balanced by a more moderate interpretation of the same event in the *Times*, February 13, 1937. Typical advertisements of rallies can be seen in *Weckruf*, February 11, April 22, 1937. Almost every box in RG 131 contains broadsides announcing rallies.
18. Leaflets advertising the Bund paper, in RG 131, Box 100; Strong, pp. 34-35.
19. *Bund*, pp. 43-44.
20. DKV leaflets, pamphlets, and trade guides, in RG 131, Boxes 90,95, and 101; *Kämpfendes Deutschtum*, 1937, p. 39; *Weckruf*, October 1, December 10, 17, 1936; May 6, November 25, December 2, 1937; *Bund*, pp. 40-41; Bund Command No. 13, September 14, 1937; No. 15, November 12, 1937; Singer (ed.), *Confidential Report*, pp. 1-8.
21. Numerous pamphlets and brochures of the Non-Sectarian Anti-Nazi League are dispersed through RG 131, especially in Boxes 93, 98, and 104; *Times*, June 28, 1937; *Weckruf*, October 1, November 12, December 10, 1936; January 28, March 11, May 13, June 10, 1937.
22. *Weckruf*, January 9, April 9, June 18, July 9, September 10, November 19, 26, 1936; October 21, December 23, 1937.
23. Bund Command No. 4, December 30, 1936.
24. Bund Command No. 5, January 5, 1937; Bund Command No. 6, January 26, 1937; Bund Command No. 7, March 15, 1937. For a general discussion of local units and the duties assigned them by national Bund headquarters, see *Un-American Propaganda*, pp. 1470-1505. This document lists four obligations of the local units to national headquarters: to create an active police unit; to organize German-American youth; to distribute the Bund newspaper; and to campaign to encourage all pro-German and anti-Jewish groups to support the DKV.
25. Bund Command No. 9, May 29, 1937; Bund Command No. 10, June 18, 1937; *Weckruf*, July 8, 1937; *Times*, July 6, 1937.

3

THE CALL
OF THE BLOOD

An extremist group always has a vision of life that is intolerant of any other. It sees itself as the whole reality, the only reality that counts. Taking cues from Nazi ideology, the Bund had such a self-centered view of life and anticipated its acceptance by large numbers of German-Americans. German racism, anti-Semitism, and anti-Communism were the main elements Bundists used to harness German-American support. Although these Nazi doctrines struck a responsive chord in Central Europe, where a long tradition of Jewish persecutions dates from the Middle Ages, in the relatively open society of the United States, free of such stigmas as the yellow badge and the body tax, the Bund's appeals were alien and unrelated to the realities of American life. Not only did most Americans, including German-Americans, find them repugnant, but when applied to concrete situations, they became fabrications devoid of meaning, expressing more rhetoric than substance.

An outstanding feature of Bund ideology was its insistence upon racism as the basis for uniting German America. Bund racism was largely an expression of pan-Germanism, and from the National Socialist point of view this meant the idea of Volksgemeinschaft: all Germans outside the Reich were united in a racial community and bound to the Fatherland by their common blood. Germans everywhere were Germans first; citizenship to a particular country took second place to the demands of blood or race.[1]

In propagating this doctrine, the Bund constantly stressed the importance of National Socialism for German-Americans. In a rather remarkable example, the pamphlet *Awake and Act*, Fritz Kuhn asserted that the Third Reich had reawakened dormant racial loyalties and sentiments among Germans everywhere. Before Hitler's rise to power, Kuhn began, German-Americans had drifted close to racial extinction, a condition resulting from "the lack of a congenial German world view." But with the "flaming words and inspiring examples" of National Socialism, he declared, the Bund would restore German-American pride and unity. As the Nazis had forged a new unity in Germany, so the Bund would create a racial alliance among all Americans of German blood.[2]

To amplify the significance of Nazism to German America, much of Bund propaganda dealt with the greatness of the Führer and the glories of National Socialist Germany. In concrete terms this involved the promotion of the Bund newspaper, *Deutscher Weckruf und Beobachter*, various pamphlets and books, and movies made in Germany. Three pamphlets received special attention: *The Snake in the Grass, Democracy or Dictatorship in Germany*; *Lifting the Pall, Germany and Hitler in Their True Light*; and *The New Germany Under Hitler.*[3] Each pamphlet was advertised in the Bund newspaper with an appeal to readers to become better informed about Germany. Each pictured Hitler as a legal and democratic statesman, who governed by majority consent. National Socialist Germany was portrayed as a nation marked by religious toleration, full employment, a just penal system, a new labor front embracing all the features of the American social security system, the elimination of alien influences, and the restoration of the old Nordic customs and traditions. Above all the Führer was represented as a man of peace, and his new Germany was interpreted as a bulwark against Communism. All of this was the familiar grist of Nazi propaganda mills.

Dull and repetitive, the Bund's campaign to create a favorable image of Hitler and Germany found further expression in the promotion of various pro-German books and actual Nazi motion pictures. Members and all German-Americans were urged to read a number of books listed under advertisements, often headed with the question, "Do you want reliable information or be treated as a moron by the promoters of anti-German propaganda?" Among the authors and titles most frequently listed were: Hitler, *Mein Kampf*; Michael Fry, *Hitler's Wonderland*; H. A. Heinz, *Germany's Hitler*; Alexander Powell, *The Long Roll on the Rhine*; Henry Albert Phillips, *Germany Today and Tomorrow*; and Theodore Fritsch, *Handbuch der Judenfrage* (Handbook on the Jewish Question). Most of these books were in English and published either in the United States or Great Britain. Orders for them were taken at national headquarters in New York.

Motion pictures provided a more entertaining and sensational type of propaganda. The Bund circulated several Nazi films to its units, including *The New Germany Introduces Itself, Hans Westmar, For Human Rights,* and *Triumph of Will.* A Bund summary of *For Human Rights* characterized the film as an excellent portrayal of Germany "during the dark November days of 1918 and the cowardly revolution."[4] The Bund also widely publicized *Triumph of Will.* In bold black print leaflets distributed on street corners carried the message:

> Adolf Hitler speaks in the mighty and spectacular sound motion picture—
> *The Triumph of Will.* Last showing Friday, May 8, 1936, 8:30 P. M. New
> York Turnhall. . . .Under the auspices of the German-American Bund.[5]

A documentary of the 1934 Nuremberg Party Rally, *Triumph of Will* is one of the most famous Nazi films. Its scenes of marching columns of troops, seas of swastikas, bonfires and torchlights, Hitler ranting to the masses, and aerial views of the Rally convey a sense of power and dynamism to the viewer.[6]

In 1936 the Bund had an opportunity to alert German-Americans to the Third Reich's most dazzling propaganda display when Germany played host to the Olympic Games. Marked by magnificent pageantry and splendid spectacles designed to impress foreign visitors, this event demonstrated to the world the new Germany's strength, faith, and hope. Throughout the spring of 1936 the Bund conducted a vigorous campaign to attract German-Americans to the Olympics in Germany. It mailed out brochures, reported on the training activities of American athletes, and attacked anti-Nazi critics in the United States who demanded that American sportsmen boycott the games. A special Olympic Edition of the *Weckruf* in June 1936 brought to its readers the Bund's view of the games. Several articles paid tribute to Hitler and argued that Germany's tremendous preparations to make the Olympics a great success merely reflected the Führer's highest political aim of establishing peaceful coopera- tion among all nations. More dramatic than this theme of Hitler as the promoter of peace was Fritz Kuhn's announcement of a Bund- sponsored trip to Germany. Kuhn reported that the Bund would present Hitler with a gift of a leather-bound *Golden Book of Ameri- can Germandom* containing signatures of members who had contri- buted at least fifty cents to Germany's Winterhilfe (Winter Relief), a Nazi charity. A special Benefit Ball held at the Yorkville Casino in New York on June 13, 1936, along with a brisk collection drive throughout the local units, netted a sum of $3,015.[7] The first page of the *Golden Book* expressed the Bund's devotion to Hitler and his principles.

> In America the hearts of the German people also beat for the great leader of all Germans. Thousands upon thousands have found new hope and faith through him and his work. The German-American Bund is the expression of his National Socialist world view. May the bonds between the German- Americans and the German people be everlasting.[8]

Exuberant promotional literature implied that German-Americans were caught by an irresistible desire to see the glorious attractions of the Third Reich. Bundists placed the experience in a religious cast comparable to a devout Moslem's pilgrimage to the Holy City of Mecca. Once in the Homeland, German-Americans would walk upon sacred German soil, mingle with people of pure German blood, and visit shrines erected to the great New Order. Overcome by these encounters, they would return to the United States emotionally and spiritually transformed, as if they had passed through a tremendous religious catharsis.

Finally, on June 23, 1936, Fritz Kuhn and over two hundred Bund members left for Germany on the liner *New York*. Amid the gaiety of deck games, coffee hours and beer evenings, Kuhn took time to write a letter to his followers in America. He wrote that the purpose of the trip was to gain strength for the struggle in the United States by seeing and experiencing Hitler's Reich. Kuhn noted that every person in the party recognized the importance of setting a good example for the Bund in Germany.

We want to tell our German brothers and sisters of our high goals and powerful work so that the Homeland can recognize that we are helping and have recognized that we are a part of the German community.[9]

In Germany, Kuhn's party was joined by another two hundred Bund members who had arrived earlier. Most of the group stayed together and toured Germany from Hamburg, through Hanover, Berlin, Cologne, Wiesbaden, Heidelberg, and Stuttgart, to Munich. In Berlin and Wiesbaden the group was met by the mayors and representatives of the VDA. In Stuttgart, Fritz Gissibl, former leader of the Friends of the New Germany, and other officials of the DAI, along with the mayor of the city, welcomed the party. At a dinner gathering Gissibl suggested that visits by Bundists to Germany should be planned each year, so that all members "working for the cause" in the United States could directly experience the Third Reich. DAI officials praised the Bund for upholding German culture in America and alerting German-Americans to the fact that their blood tied them to the greater German community. Kuhn replied that this warm reception gave him encouragement "to fight that much harder for our goals."[10]

Among the highlights of the trip was a visit to the grave of Horst Wessel, attendance at the Olympic festivals, and a march with the SA through the streets of Berlin. Overwhelmed with awe and ecstasy, one Bundist described the experience of parading through Berlin.

Thousands of people lined the streets through which the Bund marched along with the SA. Everywhere our eyes wandered there were happy, festive-minded people.... Everything was splendid.... My thoughts were back a short while—three years ago—from the Imperial Palace to the Reichs Chancellery—a torchlight procession of the SA—Germany is free. We are permitted to be proud Germans again and all of this ... we owe to one man—Adolf Hitler, the Führer of our German Homeland.[11]

The climax of the trip came on August 2, when Kuhn and a small group of Bundists met with Hitler for ten minutes at the Reichs Chancellery in Berlin. An exchange of informal greetings accompanied Kuhn's presentation of the *Golden Book* and Winterhilfe donation to Hitler, who praised the Bundesführer's work and encouraged him to "Go back and continue your fight." The audience with Hitler prompted words of reverence and rapture.

We stand before the Chancellor, the Führer of Germany. He shakes hands with
each of us, looks us straight in the eye, lays his hand on the shoulder of our
Bund leader and speaks to us of a restored Germany. He asks us about our
comrades of German blood across the sea. . . . Kuhn mentions the coming
visit to Munich; the Führer immediately takes steps to insure a warm welcome
in the city where our movement had its beginning. The Führer thanks us again
for the . . . book of testimonials and for the accompanying donation.[12]

The Olympic trip to Germany was significant for the Bund. Its
inspirational effect was most apparent. One member considered the
trip "one of the most beautiful and precious experiences of my life,"
which gave him the courage to achieve in German America what had
impressed him most in Germany—"the union of German people."
Fritz Kuhn felt strengthened by his experiences in the Reich and was
convinced that the Bund would soon "assume the political leadership
of the German element in the United States."[13]   Never again would
he be as confident and righteous as in the fall of 1936. He was
boastful about his influence in high Nazi circles and magnified the
importance of his meeting with Hitler. Photographic essays of the
Olympics and Bundists in Germany dominated the *Weckruf* for
several weeks. Many issues carried a large photograph of Kuhn
offering the *Golden Book* to Hitler. Later, when government investigations of the Bund intensified and anti-Nazi critics took the offensive, the photograph became a source of embarrassment for Kuhn.
    While in Germany, Kuhn and his party had attended the Septem-
ber 1936 Nazi Party Rally at Nuremberg. With this event Germany
inaugurated a tremendous international anti-Communist propaganda
campaign. Hitler, Goebbels, and others spoke of the underhanded
activities of an alleged international Jewish center in Moscow and
emphasized Germany's role in combating Bolshevism.[14]   After
Kuhn's return to the United States, the Bund directed a good deal of
attention to the rally, reproduced the major speeches, and for
months echoed the violent anti-Semitic invectives delivered at Nuremberg. As late as October 7, 1937, the *Weckruf* published articles
on "World Enemy No. 1—Bolshevism"; an exhibition under this title
had opened the 1936 Nuremberg Rally.
    As in all of its propaganda efforts, the Bund's anti-Communism
lacked originality; it parroted the productions of Joseph Goebbels'
fantasy factory. Its attack on Communism embraced the Nazi concept of Gesamtmarxismus (all Marxist phenomena) and masked a

virulent anti-Semitism. Bundists had visions of a vast Jewish Bolshevik conspiracy and they fought this alleged evil with a verbal ferocity matched only by the Nazi ideologist, Julius Streicher, editor of the crudely anti-Semitic weekly, *Der Stürmer*.

The Bund imagination loved the sinister plot. While attempting to explain the machinations of the international conspiracy, it moved into an incredible and mysterious realm of secret networks. It believed that the worldwide conspiracy of finance, espionage, munitions, narcotics, and politics had an efficient and rapid system of communications: a code was secretly taught to selected individuals which enabled them to wield enormous powers.

> The International Illuminati Net carries on a continuous worldwide grapevine of coded articles in the press. . . .The code-carrying articles are readily recognized by the initiated but convey nothing to the average reader. . . .So powerful. . . .has this group become through this hidden means of communication that it challenges . . . whole governments.[15]

Bundists argued that evidence for the schemes and "venom concocted" by the conspiracy could be found almost everywhere.

In sifting through the maze of Bund propaganda on anti-Communism, three themes emerge. The first was the attack on Jewish Bolshevism, with the Soviet Union taking the brunt. Stories of terror, starvation, unemployment, riots, and religious persecutions in Russia fill the Bund newspaper. Soviet Foreign Minister Maxim Litvinov came under the Bund's scrutiny in a pamphlet entitled *Litvinoff*. Advertised under the question, "Do you know this Jew?" it brought into sharp focus the Bund's connection of Jews with Communists. It set forth the argument that an alien, "preponderantly Jewish" elite not only exploited and governed the people of Russia, but was also bent on revolutionizing every nation. This document invested Litvinov with the most despicable characteristics: criminality and hate mongering and an uncontrollable lust for power coupled with personal cowardice and absolute infidelity. By masquerading as lovers of peace and democracy, the pamphlet continued, Litvinov and his "fellow racials" sought to confuse and disarm other countries. Some nations, however, saw through this propaganda and, like Germany, were becoming bulwarks against Bolshevism.[16] According to the *Weckruf* an example of aroused concern was the Anti-Comintern Pact of 1936, in which Germany, Italy, and Japan pledged to combat

Communist propaganda activities. The Bund newspaper interpreted the pact as a dramatic and constructive step toward awakening people to the dangers of the "Red world plague." The Bund's portrait of Litvinov was, of course, a vicious caricature; the charges directed at him were not true. What incensed Nazi propagandists was not so much the fact that he was Jewish as his pro-Western diplomacy. Throughout the mid- and late 1930's he tried to alert Western governments to the threat of Nazism and negotiate alliances aimed at checking German expansion.

A second theme in the Bund's anti-Communist crusade directed attention to the Nazi campaign against Gesamtmarxismus inside Germany from 1918 to 1933. National Socialist propagandists denigrated this era of the German Republic as a dismal, corrupt, and divisive period. Everything the Nazis resented was attributed by them to the Republic, frequently called "the System," an all-inclusive word covering every issue. This menace of "the System" proved too vague a concept; a more concrete enemy was needed—something irrational and restrictive, which would arouse deep-seated prejudices: the Jews of Germany provided the Nazis with this need. Since they represented a small yet articulate and prominent minority, they became the ideal scapegoat. In the propaganda drive against Gesamtmarxismus, the emphasis served to exaggerate the influence of Jews in all areas of German life. The argument was simple and clear-cut: Jews dominated the government, accounted for the cowardly foreign policies of the Weimar regime, monopolized the professions, controlled the labor unions, subsidized the agencies of public opinion, corrupted public morals, and produced degenerate art. The Jews alleged connections with Communism were stressed, with the implications that they had planned and staged several revolts. The conclusion of this diatribe exalted the National Socialist victory over German Communism and Hitler's relegation of Jews to a status appropriate to "an inferior race." With calculated scorn Jews were said to be under the full protection of the state, reconciled to National Socialism, and happier than at any other time in German history.[17]

A third theme in Bund literature transposed the Nazi view of Weimar to America. Bundists recapitulated the same characterizations in depicting the condition of American society that the National Socialists used in describing Germany prior to 1933. This contrived, stilted analysis was charged with apocalyptic overtones which warned that a society must inevitably end when cunning and depraved Jews succeeded in capturing control over all positions of influence. The analysis began with the extreme statement that the United States was "being ushered into the invisible Kingdom of Judah," a condition which had apparently developed by means of a slow and subtle process of infiltration, taking several decades to complete. Until the start of the twentieth century, Bundists lamented, America had represented a homogeneous culture based on peoples of Nordic blood, but around 1900 hordes of Jewish immigrants under all national labels were admitted to the United States. Alien to America in every way, they·did not fit into the customs and manners of American Nordics. They subverted and resisted the American heritage, undermined its Christian foundations, and gradually pushed their way into positions of authority. By the third decade of the twentieth century, continued the analysis, thousands of Jews filled key positions in federal, state, and local governments, where they maintained control over political power by means of gangster rule. Jewish politicians protected, coddled, and encouraged the activities of Jewish swindlers, gangsters, white slavers, dope peddlers, pickpockets, gunmen, and brothel keepers. If one wanted evidence of this condition of American political decadence, he could read the lurid accounts in metropolitan newspapers about Jewish gang warfare, blackmail, suicides and murders, and shady political deals.[18]

From this discussion on how Jews had captured political power the Bund outlined the effects of Jewish control over the institutions that formed public opinion. In the Bund's view, every agency of this type was under Jewish influence. As a result the United States was engulfed in a sea of Communist propaganda. Intimidated by Jewish advertisers, newspaper publishers concealed the truth about the nature of the Soviet Union and closed their columns to patriotic commentators. Jewish authority over the motion-picture industry, the theater, and radio produced a culture which lauded Jewish virtues and subversive political doctrines. Performances, jazz ballads, and popular songs of the Marx Brothers, Al Jolson, Eddie Cantor, and Irving Berlin exemplified Marxian decadence and debased and corrupted the mind. The plays of George S. Kaufman and Clifford Odets were examples of Jewish propaganda. Jewish writers manufactured a popular literature which exploited morbid sex themes and sought to undermine and destroy American patriotism and respect for past leaders and heroes.[19]

Continuing the assault on Gesamtmarxismus in the United States, Bundists contended that Jews scorned manual labor and devoted themselves to winning prominent positions in all the professions. In America as in Germany they had succeeded in this goal and thus again demonstrated their most characteristic trait: an insatiable lust for power accompanied by a demand for total subjection from all who stood in their way. Yet Jewish distaste for manual labor did not prevent the Jews forcing their will and whims on American labor unions. Indeed, Jews and their captives, such as William Green of the American Federation of Labor, held American working people in a state of bondage completely subservient to the wishes of international Communism.[20]

It was not enough, however, to claim that Jews and Communists had seized control of politics, the mass media, the professions, and the labor movement; additional references focusing upon specific acts of "Jewish arrogance" gave the attack militancy and momentum. In this regard the Bund struck at a variety of activities, twisting them into unqualified denunciations of Jewish perfidy: Jews took advantage of the free public school system to hold Communist meetings in school buildings; they indoctrinated schoolchildren with insidious propaganda and censored libraries; hundreds of Jewish businessmen in New York City defied a New York State Sunday closing law; Jews boldly asserted that the American Constitution had Hebrew origins (in Bund eyes it rested on Germanic foundations); Jews demanded that elections in New York be held on Christian but not Jewish holidays; they boycotted and picketed business establishments which supported anti-Communist movements; they openly supported the American Communist Party leader, Earl Browder, by attending his mass meetings in New York City; acting as Moscow agents, Jewish sailors sabotaged the American Merchant Marine and created disturbances every time a German ship docked in an American port.[21]

In this type of thinking there was always an element of alarm designed to frighten people with the specter of revolution, and inevitably an analogy drifted to Germany. Exactly what had happened in Germany was developing in the United States: the Jewish

Communist influence was everywhere, and soon the Communists would stage a revolution. An American Hitler was needed.

> It is true that this is becoming a nation of Jews. . . . Let there then be the hope that somewhere in America the man will come who will lead us out of this, who will do for America what Adolf Hitler has done for Germany through the National Socialist philosophy, who will bring about salvation at the last hour![22]

By drawing attention to the affairs of the alleged Jewish Communist conspiracy throughout the world and in the United States, Bundists maintained that they were demonstrating their patriotism and devotion to America. In the past, German-Americans had rendered magnificent service to their adopted country by fighting under Abraham Lincoln's banner to save the Union in a painful and bitter civil war, crusading for American progressive reforms, and sacrificing their lives for America in the World War. Now Bundists would carry this glorious tradition forward by occupying the front ranks in the battle against "culture-destroying Bolshevism."[23]

The Bund outlined several methods for combating the "Jewish rabble." A united German-American community under Bund leadership would help to contain Jewish power. The formation of Christian committees would restrict the "poisonous influence" of Jews in American public schools by demanding the right to examine all materials used in schools, placing patriotic and moral books in school libraries, and recommending patriotic speakers for student assembly programs. Bund members would continue to extend sympathy to all other American anti-Semites and would display their publications at Bund gatherings. Highly recommended were: *Pelley's Weekly, The American Gentile, Nation and Race, The Awakener, The Revealer, The Defender, James True Industrial Reports,* and *Edmondson News X-Ray.*[24]

Any literature which reflected the Bund's views received publicity. *Soviet America,* a pamphlet printed by an obsure Chicago publisher, dwelled on the necessity for America to preserve the Nordic identity of her people. This "masterly little brochure" was available at Bund national headquarters along with Henry Ford's newspaper, *The Dearborn Independent,* which contained "revealing stories about the Jews." Another favorite was the *White Knight,* the viciously anti-

Semitic newspaper of the Order of the Knights of the White Camel-
lia. The Bund believed that the appearance of so many anti-Jewish
publications constituted a reaction to Jewish control over American
newspapers and proved that American Aryans had awakened to the
seriousness of the Jewish danger, a problem that had to be solved
"either along Jewish or Aryan lines."[25]

When an American anti-Semite received what the Bund took as
unjust criticism or faced legal difficulties, the organization rallied to
his support. In the late spring of 1936 Mayor Fiorello La Guardia of
New York brought suit against Robert Edward Edmondson for libel
against the Jewish people. The Bund immediately swung into action.
It gave the event front-page coverage in the *Weckruf*, held Edmondson defense-fund rallies, and published pleas of support from Edmondson's wife. Edmondson became a martyr, an innocent man
whom the Jews intended to destroy because he fought to prevent
Communists from capturing control over the American educational
system. Surely, the Bund pleaded, Americans would not allow "the
Jewish henchmen" to sacrifice this brave man.[26]

Leaders of anti-Semitic organizations were frequent speakers at
Bund meetings. Edmondson spoke on several occasions. The founder
of the National Gentile League, Donald Shea, of Baltimore, Maryland
told a Bund audience that "the issue today is Jewism versus Gentil-
ism." On December 4, 1936, a large Bund meeting convening in
Chicago brought together representatives of Italian, German, Polish,
Ukrainian, and Russian-American organizations. Each nationality's
representative spoke on the need for all American patriots to fight
Jewish Bolshevism. A favorite speaker of the Friends of the New
Germany, self-styled anti-Semite Russell J. Dunn, harangued Bund
crowds on "How Communism Poisoned the Youth of America" and
"The Jewish Menace."[27]

During the important political year of 1936 Franklin D. Roosevelt
and the Democratic adminstration became prime targets in the German-American Bund's crusade against Jewish Bolshevism. Until the
fall of 1936, when the heat of the presidential campaign became
intense, the Bund sporadically attacked the Roosevelt adminstration
along varied lines. Some references pointed to the large number of
Jews in the adminstration, noting that FDR's brain trusters were
mostly Jews, and expressed hope that Roosevelt would rid himself of
these sinister people. Occasional articles in the *Weckruf* hinted that

Jews would tolerate Roosevelt for another four years while they worked to promote a Jew, Governor Lehman of New York, for the Democratic bid in 1940. Another source of irritation to Bundists was the WPA's Federal Theatre and the Writers' Project. They expressed alarm at the production of numerous anti-Nazi plays by the WPA project in New York—a "Moscow playhouse" supported by American taxpayers. The Writers' Project represented a concrete example of how

> Moscow-inspired doctrines of subversion manage to creep into the very arteries of American life and are enabled steadily to sap the foundation of our institutions, precisely as was the case in Germany.[28]

Speculating about the relationship of American Communist Party leader, Earl Browder, to the Roosevelt administration, Bund editors made reference to several of Browder's public speeches in which he affirmed his party's support for FDR in the 1932 election, and they raised the rhetorical question of whether the United States could effectively fight Communism under another four years of Roosevelt.[29]

In the fall of 1936 the Bund launched one of its most vulgar and vicious campaigns of hate. At times the invectives directed against Roosevelt and the Democratic administration spilled over into obscene ravings. Two issues identified as being of paramount importance to all voters were the Communist danger and the Jewish question. On the Communist issue some of the organization's charges levied against Roosevelt defy logic. One round of attack stirred prejudices: since the Communist agitated the race question, a Roosevelt victory would mean that every black male would have a white woman, and America would soon become a black republic with a black president. Another approach exaggerated the strength and magnitude of the American Communist movement, maintaining that Communists supported Roosevelt because they knew that his reelection would result in a Communist takeover of America. Roosevelt himself was responsible for this dangerous situation, since he had done nothing to alleviate revolutionary discontent or solve the problems created by the Depression. The President, who knew that the New Deal would fail, was inciting and embittering the people and thus preparing the way for a Communist revolt. The Bund sometimes dropped the calculated-plot theory and twisted the argument by suggesting that Roosevelt's own aristocratic background handicapped his ability to cope with the Depression, while Communists in the adminstration duped him into promoting catastrophic policies. In brief, whether by design or by ineptness and deception, the Bund held, Roosevelt and the New Deal had spread out the welcome mat and opened the door to Communism. This line of thinking was reinforced with a plea to all American patriots to read Elizabeth Dilling's *The Red Network*, a book which claimed that the New Deal was riddled with Communists, before voting in the November elections.[30]

Anti-Semitism was the more important ingredient in the Bund's 1936 campaign of hate. Bundists drew attention to any outstanding Jewish leader favoring a Roosevelt reelection. These endorsements were apparently proof enough of FDR's ties with powerful American Jews. It was bluntly charged that the President's Brain Trust, a Jewish Communist clique, dominated Roosevelt so firmly that America no longer had a democratic government. The United States was ruled by a Jewish dictatorship, and the Star of David most appropriately symbolized the Roosevelt administration. The *Weckruf* mocked the administration by placing names of FDR's Jewish or allegedly Jewish advisers in each section of a large Star of David. Sarcastic comments followed each name. Felix Frankfurter was labeled "the dictator of the New Deal" who had been the "Karl Marx Professor" at Harvard University before joining the New Deal. Bernard Baruch, or "Barney," became "the unofficial president" of the United States. Secretary of the Treasury Henry Morgenthau was an "international banker" bent on devaluing the dollar for the benefit of the worldwide conspiracy. Frances Perkins, the Secretary of Labor, was a "friend of aliens" and proudly declared herself a Jew. Clearly, the Bund argued, the evidence showed that the New Deal was a "Jew Deal."[31]

In mid-October 1936 the Bund publicly announced its support of the Republican candidate, Alf Landon. Fritz Kuhn took this endorsement to mean that under the Bund's guidance for the first time in American history the entire German-American community would vote as a solid block for a presidential nominee. In an attempt to translate this utopian dream into concrete reality, the Bund conducted a concerted drive to swing the German-American vote to Landon. It identified the Democratic Party as the anti-German party of war, which had humiliated Germans during the World War and, if reelected to power in 1936, would continue to persecute Germans. The *Weckruf* pleaded with German-Americans to register and vote and listed those national, state, and local candidates whom the Bund endorsed. Leaflets promoting Bund-supported candidates were distributed in New York City. Kuhn wanted every member to be aware of each candidate's special qualifications, and these were outlined and distributed to local units. Roosevelt was curtly dismissed with the usual references to Jews and Communists. No Bund member approved of his reelection.

> His preference for the Jewish element and his placing of many Jews in public office is well known. His racial policies which are opposed to those of ours are well known. . . . Besides that, his strong inclination toward the Left makes him impossible for patriotic circles. Under a new Roosevelt administration Communism would make very much progress.[32]

Kuhn heaped scorn on Union Party candidate William Lemke, labeling him a passing amusement who would shortly be forgotten. Two reasons were given for the Bund's endorsement of Landon:

> One, with a Landon victory a sharper fight against Communism . . . can be counted on, . . . Second, the election of Landon is recommended from a German standpoint because it can absolutely be assumed that under his administration more favorable commercial relations with Germany would be effected.[33]

Kuhn saw the second factor as the more important one. The Bund could best help Germany by electing a candidate who would establish important economic contacts and provide Germany with needed raw materials. The Bundesführer emphasized that the decision to support the Republican candidate was his own, free of pressure from any source in Germany or the United States.[34]

The Bund had ready-made answers to Roosevelt's tremendous election victory: the Democrats had the largest campaign fund in American history; they had successfully wooed workers and subsidized farmers and the unemployed; Roosevelt's recognition of the Soviet Union won him the support of millions of radicals. The cause of Landon's failure, however, lay elsewhere. Bundists claimed that the entire German-American community had supported Landon, but that he and other Republicans had kowtowed to American Jews.

Landon could only blame his Jewish friends and advisers for losing the contest.

> They thought more of the Jews and the Negroes and all the rest of the many colored tribes in our midst than the best elements of the country. If now they are beaten as they were never beaten before, they have only themselves to blame. They richly deserve what they got.[35]

In one sense this post-mortem was correct: more German-Americans did vote for Landon than for FDR. A Democratic administration had led the United States into the World War against Germany, and therefore many German-Americans in the 1930's still harbored suspicions that the Democratic Party was anti-German.[36] The Bund, however, never successfully exploited this sentiment. Instead, it ranted against Jews and Communists and saw enemies all around. This effort to relate the worst elements of National Socialist propaganda to the United States illustrates that the Bund had little understanding of American politics. No political movement in American history has ever succeeded in winning a mass following by propagating a foreign ideology. Bund appeals were pure and simple Nazi sloganeering, largely negative, and derived from a rush of the blood rather than a careful, critical weighing of pros and cons.

NOTES

1. An elaboration of the concept of Volksgemeinschaft can be found in Murphy, *National Socialism,* pp. 67-74, and Bischoff, *Nazi Conquest,* pp. 24-39.
2. Fritz Kuhn, *Awake and Act,* in RG 131, Box 18.
3. In RG 131, Boxes 19 and 111.
4. *Weckruf,* November 26, 1936.
5. Bund leaflets in RG 131, Boxes 13 and 121.
6. Siegfried Kracauer gives a good analysis of "Triumph of Will" in *From Caligari to Hitler,* pp. 300-303.
7. *Weckruf,* June 18, 1936; Rogge, *Official German Report,* p. 119.
8. *Weckruf,* July 23, 1936.
9. *Weckruf,* August 13, 1936.
10. *Weckruf,* September 10, October 1, 1936.
11. *Kämpfendes Deutschtum,* 1937, pp. 55-56.
12. Ibid.
13. Ibid.; Bund Command No. 1, October 28, 1936.
14. Zeman, *Nazi Propaganda,* pp. 89-95; Burden, *The Nuremberg Party Rallies: 1923-1939,* pp. 121-136.

15. *Weckruf*, September 23, 1937.
16. Andersen, *Litvinoff*, in RG 131, Box 104.
17. *The New Germany Under Hitler*, in RG 131, Box 111, pp. 25-26; *Weckruf*, August 27, October 29, 1936; February 18, September 23, 1937.
18. *Weckruf*, February 6, 13; April 30, May 28, August 27, 1936; October 28, 1937.
19. *Weckruf*, February 27, April 30, June 4, August 12, October 1, 1936.
20. *Weckruf*, July 15, August 20, September 3, November 26, 1936.
21. *Weckruf*, January 23, February 6, April 16, October 29, 1936; January 28, June 17, July 22, October 28, 1937.
22. *Weckruf*, July 16, 1936.
23. *Kämpfendes Deutschtum*, 1937, p. 51
24. *Weckruf*, February 27, August 27, 1936; October 28, 1937; Strong, *Organized Anti-Semitism*, analyzes some of the organizations represented by these newspapers.
25. *Weckruf*, February 13, September 3, 1936; February 11, March 11, 1937.
26. *Weckruf*, June 18, 1936. The plaintiffs dropped the case when they decided that their charge against Edmondson for libeling Jews provided a weak basis for legal action. The Bund interpreted this result as a great victory for American justice.
27. *Weckruf*, December 17, 1936; September 16, 1937. Numerous leaflets announcing Dunn's addresses to Bund meetings are scattered throughout RG 131; some are in Boxes 95, 110, and 112.
28. *Weckruf*, February 20, 1936.
29. *Weckruf*, May 28, June 4, July 2, 16; September 17, 1936.
30. *Weckruf*, September 3, 17, 24; October 22, 1936.
31. *Weckruf*, September 10, 17, 24; October 8, 29, 1936.
32. Bund Command No. 2, October 29, 1936.
33. Ibid.
34. Ibid.
35. *Weckruf*, November 12, 1936.
36. Gerson, *The Hyphenate in Recent American Politics and Diplomacy*, pp. 33, 119-120.

4

"WE MUST WELCOME
EVERY FIGHT"

The German-American Bund reached the zenith of its power and influence in 1937 and 1938. Recruitment drives brought in new members, the number of local units increased, and the American press gave wide coverage to the organization's activities.[1] Not all was gain, however. The Bund's self-portrayal as an organization ready and eager for combat, its boisterous affairs, its obvious Nazi character and sympathies, all provoked alarm, suspicion, and often sharp and hostile criticism from numerous Americans. The year 1937 offered Bundists an opportunity to battle as it witnessed the beginnings of an extended series of attacks on and investigations of Bund affairs by private, state, and federal agencies. Every attack produced an outburst of indignation and spurred Bundists to exploit the controversies surrounding their movement with propaganda, verbal abuse against their opponents, mass rallies, and agitation in the streets. Like the Nazis in Germany during the 1920's, they relished the growing intensity of the opposition, viewing it as good publicity for the movement.

The beginnings of significant opposition to the German-American Bund coincided with a general hardening of American attitudes toward Nazi Germany. By 1937 all the major power groups in the United States—including the labor, business, religious, and intellectual communities—had condemned the Third Reich.[2] Long before this time, however, Congressman Samuel Dickstein of New York, the most persistent opponent of American National Socialism, had carried on a personal crusade against Nazism. As the Bund drew more public attention and made clear its sympathies for the Third Reich, he concentrated on alerting the public to the potential dangers of permitting Bundists to ape Nazi ways and to spread foreign propaganda. A Russian Jew who migrated to America around the turn of the century, Dickstein seemingly offered Bundists a concrete example of the international Jewish Communist conspiracy. Therefore they directed at him the most atrocious verbal violence. He was tagged "the ghetto Congressman," a mentally deranged individual suffering from a Nazi persecution mania or "Hitleritis." Bundists were irritated by Dickstein's proposal for the creation of a House Un-American Activities Committee to investigate Nazism in the United States. Though this measure was voted down in April 1937, in late June the New York Congressman became the champion of a resolution introduced by Representative Martin Dies of Texas providing for an investigation of subversive activities. In support of this cause Dickstein published several lists of alleged Nazi spies in America in the *Congressional Record*, naming Kuhn and other Bundists as active agents of the Third Reich. He attacked Bund camps as secret Nazi centers, where foreign agents trained to overthrow the American government.[3] The New York Congressman was a formidable opponent, and the Bund could not cavalierly ignore him. He had co-chaired the McCormick Committee of 1934 which, in part, had contributed to the breakup of the Friends of the New Germany.

In facing Dickstein's assaults, Fritz Kuhn steeled the Bund for battle, exhorting members never to forget that "as a fighting organization we must welcome every fight." He outlined a plan designed to deluge Washington with letters affirming the Bund's loyalty to America. No names were mentioned, but Kuhn claimed that national headquarters would send letters to various senators, congressmen, Supreme Court justices, governors, national leaders of the Republican and Democratic parties, important commanders of the Army and Navy, and national officers of the American Legion and Veterans of Foreign Wars. Unit leaders were to perform the same task on the local level by writing to state legislators, mayors, local officials of the major political parties, state, county and city judges, other important community leaders, newspapers, officials of the National Guard, and

American patriotic organizations. Members and sympathizers were asked to send contributions to a special fighting fund created to finance this campaign. In line with Kuhn's directive, the *Weckruf* aimed venomous verbal broadsides at Dickstein and gave careful instructions to readers on how to write a letter of protest to congressmen: they should use good English, be sure of their facts, and avoid using the term "Nazi." Having alerted the organization, Kuhn sent a telegram to Speaker of the House of Representatives William B. Bankhead, expressing indignation over Dickstein's statements and welcoming a federal investigation of the Bund. The Bundesführer also directed an open letter to Congress which questioned Dickstein's sanity and categorically denied his charges against the Bund. Under the slogan "Come and Hear Our Answer to Dickstein and the Jewish Rabble Rousers" several mass rallies were staged in New York.[4] All this vigorous activity was a demonstration of the Bund's incendiarism at its height. The saturation of the mails with protest letters, the appeal for finances, the drive to contact community leaders, and the mass rallies amounted to a striking display of energy, dedication, and zeal.

In the summer of 1937 thousands of people were attracted to Camps Siegfried and Nordland, where the Bund staged sensational displays of demagoguery complemented with the outward trappings of Nazism. OD and youth groups marched; Bund leaders spoke on how Jewish Communism poisoned the minds of youth. Usually the rallies ended with the singing of the "Horst Wessel Song" and repeated "Sieg Heils." Dickstein had expressed concern over camp affairs, and as the weeks wore on, an increasing number of individuals and organizations echoed his warnings. The Non-Sectarian Anti-Nazi League, a militant organization devoted to alerting the public about the menace of National Socialism, sent telegrams to the US Attorney General, several senators, congressmen, and labor leaders requesting an immediate investigation and closing of Bund camps. Commanders of local New Jersey units of the American Legion and Veterans of Foreign Wars called for the immediate dissolution of the Bund with deportation of its leaders, made arrangements for private detectives to conduct probes about Nordland, and demanded a congressional investigation. Other veteran groups sent protests to President Roosevelt and New Jersey representatives condemning camp activities, especially the practice of displaying the swastika.

Congressmen William M. Citron of Connecticut and Fred A. Hartley of New Jersey asked for an FBI inquiry. The Bund responded to this clamor by threatening to sell the camps to Negroes. From the rostrums at Siegfried and Nordland, Fritz Kuhn lambasted Dickstein and other critics of his movement. The Bundesführer referred to Dickstein's list of Nazi spies as "a roll call of the dead and missing"; the veterans opposing the Bund were "puppets of the subversive Zionist wire-pullers." He stressed the theme of a persecuted German-American element. In 1917 all German-Americans had suffered from discrimination and humiliation; and now they were threatened again, for assaults on the Bund were attacks on German-Americans generally.⁵ As the Bund worked in an increasingly hostile environment, Kuhn repeatedly made this parallel. Though it was a passionate appeal to German-Americans, it nevertheless failed. The hysteria of the World War I era was not repeated; the Bund alone came under scrutiny, not German America.

In mid-August 1937, US Attorney General Homer S. Cummings announced that the FBI had started an investigation of Bund camps to determine if any violated federal laws. Kuhn ostensibly welcomed this action, claiming that his movement had nothing to hide. But again he raised the cry of persecution. To be sure, he reasoned, German-Americans came under the jurisdiction of the FBI, as did murderers, gangsters, counterfeiters, rapists, and all outlaws from society. But although he publicly assumed a confident attitude, Kuhn gave careful instructions to unit leaders. Members must hold no irresponsible conversations with strangers; identification papers of government agents must be carefully studied; and questions concerning the size and strength of the Bund were to be parried; the local leadership must emphasize to the public that the Bund had no official ties with Germany; President Roosevelt must not be verbally attacked; and only Bund leaders could issue statements to the press. Moreover, the Bundesführer provided ready-made answers to possible questions of government investigators regarding the subsidiary organizations. For example, the role of the OD was to preserve order at meetings and stand ready to place itself at the disposal of the government in the event of an emergency. The camps were places of recreation, where young people enjoyed sports and older people assembled to picnic and share common views. The *Weckruf* was the chief organ of the Bund and reflected a friendly and sympathetic attitude toward Germany. The DKV acted as an economic self-protective agency in combating the movement to boycott German goods. Finally, Kuhn stressed that the Bund was an American organization, working within the framework of the law, which saw as its main task the abolishment of Jewish Communist influence.⁶ Kuhn's usual defense—the claim that the Bund represented an American movement—never convinced many Americans, who took due cognizance of the Bund's propagation of a foreign ideology, glorification of Hitler, and display of the swastika and other Nazi regalia.

Throughout the fall of 1937 adversaries of the Bund persisted in their warnings and efforts to contain the organization's activities. Its camp affairs continued to arouse anxieties: a convention of New Jersey American Legionnaires adoped a resolution opposing the establishment of Bund camps; a justice of the peace in Yaphank, Long Island—a village near Camp Siegfried—suggested arming local citizens against possible Nazi aggression. When the Bund purchased a 178-acre site near Southbury, Connecticut, for the purpose of establishing a camp, a gathering of enraged townspeople and farmers produced a resolution denouncing the Bund camps as un-American foreign agencies. Local ministers alluded to the Bund as "this un-Christian, un-American insidious menace." While Bundists cleared scrub trees from the grounds of their projected camp site, local constables arrested them under an old blue law forbidding work on Sunday. The Bund finally abandoned the proposal after the town council of Southbury revised a zoning code which would fine Bundists up to $250 a day if they continued the camp project.⁷

American anti-Nazis occasionally used radio broadcasts to convey their message. On November 18, 1937, for example, Stefan Heym, a freelance author and playwright who edited a liberal German-American newspaper, *Deutsches Volksecho*, delivered an address over station WIP, New York, on Nazi activities in the United States. He warned that the German-American Bund was a threat to America, charging that its camps were Nazi training grounds where children learned race hatred and sang songs preaching murder. Heym said that Bundists might be preparing for a putsch but concluded that the great mass of German-Americans loathed Nazism and were uniting with patriotic Americans to stamp out its threat to democracy.⁸ Other individuals spoke out against American National Socialism. The National Commander of the American Legion, Harry W. Colmery, called Nazism a peril to democracy; John L. Spivak, a popular writer and journalist, testified before a special committee of the Massachusetts Legislature investigating Nazi, fascist, Communist, and Ku Klux Klan activities in the Bay State that a vast Nazi propaganda apparatus existed in America functioning through native fascist groups as well as through the Bund.

A particularly irksome incident arose in late November 1937 when Judge J. Wallace Leyden of Hackensack, New Jersey, declared to a group of German-Americans in naturalization court that membership in the German-American Bund was sufficient ground for denying citizenship. Although the judge did not refuse to grant citizenship to anyone, the Bund took his remarks very seriously and immediately swung into action. Kuhn published an open letter to him and other government officials; editorals in the *Weckruf* expressed astonishment at the judge's position and argued that German-Americans should not be penalized for revering Adolf Hitler as the savior of the Homeland. A few days after Judge Leyden's statement appeared in the press, the Bund held a mass rally in Hackensack during which inflammatory speeches were directed at him.[9]

Despite all opposition, Bundists ended 1937 in an aggressive and confident mood. Brooding over discouraging events was not part of the Bund identity. In their simplistic view of the world the problems confronting their organization came from only one source: Jewish agents stood behind every assault, from Dickstein's attempt to start a congressional inquiry to Judge Leyden's declaration that membership in the Bund was valid grounds for denying American citizenship. Bundists boasted that hereafter they would return blow for blow. In his end-of-year messages to the units Kuhn noted only briefly that Dickstein lacked the holiday spirit and that Jews abused American political freedoms by slandering those who disagreed with them. The Bundesführer devoted most of his attention to the economic achievements of the Third Reich, claiming that Germans would be far happier this Christmas than they had been a decade earlier. Kuhn looked forward to the new year, seeing hope and promise but also more hard work and struggle. He urged local leaders to move with him into 1938 with courage and cooperation.[10]

On January 5, 1938, U.S. Attorney General Homer S. Cummings informed a press conference in Washington, D.C. of the results of an FBI investigation of the German-American Bund. Kuhn's confidence and optimism seemed justified, for the Attorney General announced that the Bund had not violated any federal law, nor had FBI Director J. Edgar Hoover found evidence which warranted legal action against the organization. Bundists were jubilant over this report; they viewed it as a turning point in the history of their movement. If Dickstein and all of "the sons of Zion" were to raise the cry of Nazism again, they would be laughed into political oblivion: the entire United States knew that the Bund was not a subversive society. Kuhn instructed local leaders to ignore investigators, send to national headquarters all newspaper accounts of the FBI report, and discuss its findings with members. On one matter, however, Kuhn made a concession to the opposition. The intensely hostile American reaction to the Bund's display of the swastika prompted him to design a new organizational flag which emphasized the letters "AV," signifying Amerika-Deutscher Volksbund, and placed the swastika in an inconspicuous position. Hereafter the new banner would be displayed at all public events, while the swastika would appear with the American flag to decorate halls and camps." This decision marked the first in a number of modifications Bundists made in an effort to stem criticism of their movement.

Encouraged by the Justice Department's report, Bundists launched 1938 with a campaign to expand the circulation of the *Weckruf* and to win new members. Cash commissions totaling $5,000 and prizes including a car, refrigerators, and radios were offered as incentives to individuals to sell new subscriptions to the newspaper. Kuhn sent G. Wilhelm Kunze, Bund publicity director, on a speaking tour throughout the eastern and midwestern Gaue for the purpose of recruiting new members. Kunze was given the authority to create new units, and local leaders were urged to advertise his visit and to invite both American and German outsiders, so that large crowds appeared wherever he spoke. This campaign to expand Bund membership was accompanied by more energetic efforts. On January 30, 1938, the Bund held a mass rally at New York's Turnhalle to celebrate the anniversary of the founding of the Third Reich. On the same evening angry representatives of various anti-Nazi organizations gathered in Carnegie Hall to protest five years of dictatorship in Germany. Bund editorials commenting on these events allotted more space to the anti-Nazi demonstration than to its own affair. For one night, the *Weckruf* reported, Carnegie Hall became a synagogue filled with thousands of Jews and "their Aryan train-bearers," who raised noise and hot air.[12]

Loud shouts and emotional oratory continued to characterize anti-Nazi activity, and a few violent incidents occurred. A bomb exploded outside a building in Philadelphia where the local Bund unit held business meetings. In Buffalo, New York, a riot squad intervened to end a fist fight between American Legion members and Bundists. This violence was accompanied by threatening rhetoric. Labor organizations of Reading, Pennsylvania, warned that they would take whatever steps necessary to stop the Bund from establishing a camp in their district. American veteran groups in New Milford, New Jersey, made similar threats to prevent Bundists from using public meeting halls. No single one of these events was important, but when juxtaposed with the Bund's blatant pro-Nazi affairs and the rising tide of American anti-Nazi activity, the incidents took on considerable significance. Official diplomatic circles in Washington and Berlin began to express a growing anxiety over Kuhn's organization. The American Ambassador to Germany, William E. Dodd, not only made his antipathy to Nazi views well known, but also charged that the Bund was a Nazi organ linked to German agencies. His successor, Hugh Wilson, was more discreet, and along with Prentiss Gilbert, the American chargé d'affaires in Berlin, complained to the German Foreign Ministry about the Nazi activities of German nationals in the United States. Hans Dieckhoff, the German Ambassador in Washington, looked disapprovingly at American National Socialism and throughout 1937 and 1938 sent reports to Berlin stressing the damage wrought to German-American relations by the Bund's "stupid and noisy activities." While commending Bundists for their aggressive defense of National Socialist Germany and their fight against Jews and Communists, he outlined several factors which had a debilitating effect on the Bund's effort: it received negative press publicity; its emulation of the Nazi Party's forms and ideology angered Americans; and its members had no roots or influence in the United States and therefore could not function realistically in American politics. Of the utmost significance, the German Ambassador continued, was the fact that German America was not an element capable of being exploited for Germany's benefit. Not only was it a dwindling, weak, and divided community, but the majority of German-Americans had no consciousness of being German. Dieckhoff cited figures from the Chicago German-American community to buttress his argument: of the 700,000 people of German descent in the area, about 40,000 had an awareness of a German identity, and of these only 450 belonged to the Bund. In view of this situation, he recommended that German citizens be forced to resign from the Bund and that all political contacts between German authorities and the Bund be stopped. Dieckhoff's repetitive and forceful protests had important results. The German consulate in New York urged the Bund to modify its program, and on March 1, 1938, Berlin made public a statement prohibiting German nationals from membership in the German-American Bund and the Prospective Citizens League.[13] This announcement was a restatement of a similar proclamation, issued in December 1935, which had led many German nationals to return to Germany, thus decimating the ranks of the Friends of the New Germany. At Bund headquarters in New York officials tried to minimize the importance of Berlin's decree by boasting that they took orders from no one. Yet the leadership was worried, and in early March 1938 Kuhn went to Germany to appeal the decision. In a conversation with Fritz Wiedemann, Hitler's adjutant, Kuhn demanded a reconsideration of the question, but Wiedemann remained intransigent; he told the Bundesführer that his fumbling imitations of the party in America had strained German-American relations.[14] This rebuff appeared to have little effect on Kuhn, who later ignored the March decree by permitting German nationals to remain in his movement. More damaging to his interests were his boasts of alleged meetings in Berlin with Goebbels and Goering; although this fabrication may have enhanced his position within the organization, American press accounts of his statements helped strengthen the public image of the Bund as a Nazi agency.

In March 1938 Germany's sensational move into Austria turned the organization's concern to foreign affairs. The Bund's coverage of foreign events always faithfully echoed and pursued the aims of Nazi propagandists; throughout 1937 and early 1938 two themes emerged. On the one hand, in keeping with its goal of weakening the United States' opposition to German policies, the Bund called for American neutrality and isolation from European matters. This theme was developed along several lines. Bundists praised the efforts of such outstanding American isolationists as Senator Gerald Nye. They publicized a Gallup Poll of 1937 which showed that 70 percent of the individuals polled thought that American entry into the World War had been a mistake. President Roosevelt's Quarantine Speech of October 5, 1937—warning that America could expect difficulties if aggression went unchecked throughout the world—became the subject of *Weckruf* editorials. FDR's address was interpreted as an act designed to spread war hysteria, and readers were cautioned that "the folly of 1917" would be repeated unless Americans woke up and urged their leaders to stay out of European entanglements. Bundists called for the passage of the Ludlow proposal, one of the most striking manifestations of American isolationist sentiment, providing for a national referendum on declarations of war except in the case of invasion. When it met defeat, Bundists remarked that international bankers, munitions makers, and "the kept press" had won another victory. On the other hand, while supporting and exploiting American isolationism, the Bund attempted to justify every act related to German diplomacy. It criticized the 1919 Versailles settlement, lauded conditions inside Germany, vindicated German rearmament, and issued pro-Franco reports on the Spanish Civil War along with scathing attacks on the Soviet Union.[15]   Later, in 1940 and 1941, after war had broken out on the Continent and the Bund was struggling to survive, the major thrust of these themes changed. Though glorification of Hitler's Germany and diplomacy continued, it was put in a low key, the main emphasis being on the need for American neutrality.

In early 1938 Nazi propaganda mills dwelled extensively on foreign press misrepresentations of events occurring in Germany. When Hitler spoke on this subject before the German Reichstag on February 20, 1938, the Bund newspaper carried excerpts from his speech and for weeks struck at the foreign press as the vehicle of international warmongering. On March 11, 1938, German troops marched across the Austro-German border, and within a few hours Austria became part of the Third Reich. American press reaction to the Anschluss was extremely hostile, and in response Bundists cried misrepresentation. They argued that American newspapers were making a frantic effort to discredit Germany by interpreting the Austrian event as a rape, a crime against civilization, an invasion of a helpless little country by a brutal dictator. Bundists insisted that only the *Weckruf* published the truth and pointed to dispatches from Austria which reported a hysterically enthusiastic welcome for Hitler's entry into Vienna. Germany had committed no wrong; she had instead realized and fulfilled the "dream of 1000 years" for Germandom. In the months following Hitler's move into Austria the *Weckruf* printed numerous articles on the benefits to the Austrians of the union of Germany and Austria by the establishment of new industries, a public-works program, and relief measures for the poor. Further justification of the act compared it to the American annexation of Texas and rephrased Hitler's favorite rationale for expansion—the self-determination of the German people.

Although the United States administration expressed disapproval, official Washington did not become involved in the Austrian affair. Dieckhoff's dispatches to Berlin reported that rage had overcome the State Department and that the American press indulged in "a fantastic hate campaign" over the Anschluss. The Ambassador warned his superiors that the Third Reich could not expect American sympathy or neutrality in the event of a large-scale war between Germany and the Western democracies. In such a conflict, he predicted, America would support Great Britain.[16] Dieckhoff's observations on the hostile American reaction to the Anschluss were equally applicable to the Bund. The weeks following the events in Central Europe witnessed continued expressions of anti-Nazi outrage against the Bund. J. Parnell Thomas, a New Jersey congressman who was disturbed by the Austrian events, suggested calling out the state militia to close down Bund camps. At Trenton, New Jersey, and Philadelphia, Pennsylvania, near-riots developed when G. Wilhelm Kunze attempted to speak before Bund gatherings. Hundreds of anti-Nazis booed him off the stage, forcing him to leave the halls by a side entrance while police protected him from hostile mobs milling around outside. Opponents of the Bund increased their organizational efforts. On April 3, 1938, a federation of German-American clubs met in convention at Newark, New Jersey, and mapped out plans to win the cooperation of veteran, civic, and religious organizations in an effort to combat Nazi propaganda. About a week later, the Non-Sectarian Anti-Nazi League brought together delegates from twenty-three trade unions and Catholic, Jewish, and Protestant groups at the Hotel Astor in New York for the purpose of creating a national movement to battle the "organized menace of Nazism in the United States."[17]

On almost every weekday night throughout the early spring of

1938 the Bund managed carefully prepared and widely advertised mass rallies in New York. The largest of these affairs took place on the evening of April 20, when a crowd of 3,500 people gathered at the Yorkville Casino to celebrate Hitler's forty-ninth birthday. Unknown to the Bund, one hundred American Legion members were in the audience. As the opening speaker remarked that the Anschluss was Hitler's birthday present to Germany, a man arose and shouted "Is this an American or German meeting?" Immediately the hall became the scene of a wild uproar with shouts of "throw him out" followed by a free-for-all fist fight between OD men and Legionnaires. The Yorkville Casino riot produced several badly beaten victims and aroused indignant protests from both anti-Nazi groups and the Bund. Tempers and emotions over the Yorkville riot had hardly cooled when another violent incident occurred. Four youths invaded the Brooklyn office of Charles Weiss, editor of the anti-Nazi, anti-Communist magazine *Uncle Sam*, beat him into semiconsciousness when he refused to kiss a German flag, and scratched swastika emblems on his back and chest. The attackers were never identified as Bundists, but anti-Nazis drew what seemed to them the logical conclusion—the beating of Weiss was the work of "Bund thugs." For several days after the violent events in Yorkville and Brooklyn, police took extraordinary precautions to guard Bund meetings. When, for example, on April 24, 500 Bundists traveled by train from Manhattan to White Plains, New York, to hold a rally, special police units and a member of the bomb squad went with them, while other policemen stood guard on rooftops and at stations along the route. Police officers occasionally cancelled Bund rallies if a threat of violence seemed imminent.[18]

In April 1938, just after his unsuccessful trip to Germany, Kuhn issued an angry reply to the sharp criticisms and violent acts directed at his movement. In the pages of the *Weckruf* he once again affirmed that the Bund held no divided allegiance: it stood committed to America and demanded the same rights and privileges given to any other American organization. He warned that what had happened in Yorkville would occur again if unwanted "Jewish strangers" invaded Bund rallies. These celebrations, he insisted, were of interest to German-Americans only, and the "Communist provocatuers" who attempted to disrupt the affairs had received the beating they deserved. Kuhn denied Bund involvement in the Weiss case, commenting, "we have yet to hear of a Nazi who would permit a Jew to kiss the swastika even if he wanted to!"[19] The Bundesführer's public defiance was followed by a belligerent directive to local leaders in which he said nothing about his cool reception in Germany but noted that the Anschluss had given him new strength; his observations of anti-Communist movements in Europe had convinced him that the Bund was also on the correct course, moving progressively forward. The intense attacks on the organization, Kuhn believed, simply proved that "opponents respect and fear us." He then outlined some basic guidelines on which, he maintained, the Bund would either rise or fall. Hereafter records of all American citizens admitted to Bund membership must contain the date citizenship was received and the address of the court where the oath was administered. Kuhn violated Berlin's decree of March 1, by announcing the continuation of the Prospective Citizens League. Members of the League would continue to assume the duties and enjoy the rights and privileges of full Bund membership, but other than cultural, educational, DKV, and youth offices, they could not hold leadership positions. On the subject of sympathizers, Kuhn noted that any Aryan, irrespective of nationality, could become a sympathizer by donating the regular monthly dues of 75 cents. Such an individual neither held a membership card nor participated in meetings, but Kuhn urged unit leaders to attract people who wanted to support the movement yet who for some personal, political, or economic reason could not openly commit themselves. He instructed unit leaders to avoid connections with German consulates or other Reich officials except on such special celebrations as Hitler's birthday or Reich Anniversary Day, when the German representative should be invited. The Bundesführer recommended that each local unit rent a post-office box under the code name AVAU for correspondence between national headquarters and the unit. This device would provide a measure of security and keep the addresses of local units from falling into enemy hands. Kuhn closed his message with a plea for discipline among rank-and-file members.

> Our Bund movement has been injured by too much softness and a tendency to yield. The sharpness of the struggle is of such a nature that we cannot allow ourselves to become complacent. I demand, therefore, the unceasing support of every Bund member for carrying through the führer principle . . . as the only indispensable guarantee of the strength of our movement.[20]

Critics of the Bund likewise became inflexible. Representative Dickstein stiffened his attacks by speaking out against Kuhn's group over the radio, urging local communities to ban Bund gatherings. He spoke of "sensational revelations" which he planned to present to an investigating committee that Congress would soon create. Representative Hamilton Fish of New York introduced a bill in the House providing for measures to curb any private army—a euphemism for the Bund's OD. In early May 1938 the New York Commander of Disabled War Veterans, Roy P. Monahan, initiated a legal suit against six officials of the German-American Settlement League (the Bund corporation controlling Camp Siegfried) for allegedly violating a New York State law requiring oath-bound organizations to submit a membership roster to the New York Secretary of State. This complaint was brought to court after Monahan's organization had spent several months investigating Camp Siegfried. As a result, the six officials were arrested and released on $1,000 bail each, pending a jury trial. For the Bund, this growing opposition, especially the legal action taken against Siegfried, was "more Red-Jewish hate breeding." A *Weckruf* report on the matter pointed to a familiar pattern: a Jew inspired by hate and vindictiveness brought charges against an innocent Bund member; the newspapers blew up the story, and after several postponements the judge dismissed the defendant while the press deliberately avoided mentioning the outcome. Behind this proceeding, the report concluded, stood "Red Jews and their ilk," who feared the Bund because it was arousing America to the threat they presented to the country. Fritz Kuhn sent telegrams to President Roosevelt, Attorney General Cummings, and Speaker of the House Bankhead requesting an investigation of the "pseudo patriots attacking us." At a mass rally in New York, heavily guarded by police, he announced that the Bund would accept any challenge and looked forward to a showdown.[21]

A showdown did in fact appear imminent on May 26, when debate opened in the House on a resolution, sponsored by Representative Martin Dies of Texas and strongly supported by Dickstein, calling for a new investigation of un-American activities. A two-hour debate produced heated arguments assailing Nazism and Communism. At one point Dies spoke of shocking activities occurring in Bund camps, claiming that a speaker had called for the assassination of the President. This time the measure passed, and on June 6 appointments to the House Un-American Activities Committee were made. Although Dickstein had supplied much of the pressure for the creation of this inquiry, he was not selected as a committee member; he was apparently held to be too zealous a partisan by midwestern congressmen, who believed him to be anti-German. The Bund was not unduly worried about the committee: its members were tagged "Dickstein's caddies" out to suppress the German-American element in an effort to transfer more political power to Jews. Kuhn sent a telegram to Dickstein: "My sincerest condolences on your political funeral. Am sorry you are not on the Dies Committee because I lose the opportunity to finish you in one round."[22]

The Bund could afford general indifference to the House Committee; in the summer of 1938 it ignored American Nazism and became the sounding board for charges of domestic communist infiltration. A new challenge, however, came from a New York State investigating committee chaired by State Senator John J. McNaboe, which opened hearings on the Bund in New York City on June 22, 1938.[23] Responding to a subpoena, Kuhn wrote to McNaboe that he and other officials of the organization would be happy to appear before the committee to explain the patriotic aims and purposes of the Bund. McNaboe quizzed Bund officials for three days and failed to uncover anything new about American Nazism. The dialogue between Bundists and the Senator produced only exasperating repetitive questioning followed by tart, terse answers and hisses from the audience. McNaboe probed Kuhn about the meaning of the swastika, the Nazi salute, and a photograph showing Kuhn and other Bundists meeting Hitler. Inevitably the questions drifted to the Bund's anti-Semitism. Kuhn insisted that Jews were enemies of America, and the Senator discussed the fallacies of his remarks to no avail; the Bundesführer remained adamant. Committee member Assemblyman Irwin Steingut argued with other Bundists who declared that a state of war existed in the United States between Aryans and Jews. When Steingut asked one Bundist to name the most important members of the Roosevelt adminstration, he could only reply that they were all Jews. The *Weckruf* front-page report on Kuhn's appearance before the McNaboe committee referred to the investigation as "an inquisition" and implied that Kuhn had handled himself magnificently before a crowd of people "stamped with dark Hebraic features." The fact that so few Aryans sat in the audience had a disquieting effect on

McNaboe, leading him to attach too much importance to insignificant matters. Yet this "Jewish-instigated" investigation, the report concluded, had not compromised the Bund and only proved once again that the organization was 100 percent American. On the other hand the New York *Times'* coverage of the McNaboe proceedings pointed to the arrogance of Bund witnesses, their raucous anti-Semitism, and their obvious affection for Hitler.[24]

By mid-1938 the New York *Times* was not alone in its caustic reportage of Bund affairs. Numerous national magazines—such as *The Nation, The New Republic,* and *Ken*—joined the anti-Bund chorus by publishing biting articles on American Nazism.[25] On the West Coast, the Los Angeles *Times,* the Los Angeles *Examiner,* and the Los Angeles *Evening Herald and Express,* as well as the San Francisco *Examiner,* the San Francisco *Chronicle,* the Seattle *Star,* and the Spokane *Press* dealt extensively with Bund events, and for good reason. Herman Schwinn, leader of the Western Gau, openly admitted that he was a National Socialist and vigorously barnstormed the area from Seattle, Washington, to San Diego, California, to promote the Nazi cause. A former insurance salesman, Schwinn's repulsive manner, his anti-Semitic venom, his continual references to his German shepherd Lump, who, he boasted, was trained to attack any Jew gave western Bundists a notorious reputation and spurred anti-Nazis to counterattack. A typical clash occurred on May 30, 1938, when Schwinn presided over a Pacific Coast Bund convention in San Francisco. Here one thousand Bundists and a few units of William D. Pelley's Silver Shirts, a native fascist organization, held sessions inside California Hall while outside three thousand anti-Nazis picketed, jeered, booed, threw rocks at the building windows, and carried placards reading "Drive the Nazis Out of Town." Schwinn told the delegates that America was fighting a second war of independence, this time against international Jewry and Communism, and that America's economic problems would not be ended until the Jewish problem was solved. It would be difficult, he claimed, to resolve the Jewish question, since "pink and red Jews" had infiltrated the Roosevelt adminstration. The San Francisco *Call Bulletin* commented that the convention was an "invasion" of the city by "Nazi followers" and "Hitlerites" who represented a serious threat to American institutions.[26]

The constant unfavorable publicity given by the press to the Bund was a liability American-Nazis were never able to change. Even more damaging to their long-range interests was a series of legal problems. The first significant legal action taken against the Bund began in early July 1938, when the six officials of the German-American Settlement League, arrested early in May, and the League itself went on trial at Riverhead, Long Island. The case for the prosecution hinged on proving that the Bund represented an oath-bound organization. If this point could be verified the defendants faced possible imprisonment and fines for violating a New York State law holding all oath-bound societies responsible for filing a membership list with the Secretary of State. Prosecution attorneys announced that a victory at this trial would be followed by similar court action against all Bund leaders. Their case rested on the testimony of Willy Brandt, an ex-Nazi and Bundist, who declared that he had joined the SA in Germany in 1930, migrated to the United States a few years later, and joined the Bund in May 1938. Upon accepting membership in the Bund, Brandt swore, he had to take an oath of loyalty to Adolf Hitler and Bund leaders. The defense brought twenty-five people to the witness stand, most of them American-born rank-and-file Bund members, and each testified that an oath was not required for membership. James Wheeler-Hill, National Secretary of the Bund, produced a letter for the defense which alleged that Brandt had been denied admission to the organization. The testimony of the defense witnesses should have led the jury to question Brandt's integrity, but the obnoxious manner of these individuals influenced the final verdict more than did concrete evidence. They proudly flaunted their anti-Semitism—one proclaiming that all Jews were criminals and Communists, another that Jews had haunted him all his life, forcing him to move from one job to another. Under cross-examination by a prosecuting attorney, several Bundists ignored the questions and shouted that the Nazi salute would be adopted by all Americans in the near future or that Hitler's name was too great to be thrown about in a courthouse. This behavior, coupled with the noisy demonstrations from a courtroom filled with Bundists, led the judge to comment that he had seen things happen in this court which he did not believe could occur in America. After four days of testimony the jury took less than fifteen minutes to deliver a guilty verdict. The judge gave the maximum penalty in each case, the League being fined $1,000 and each defendant $500. He imposed a one-year jail sentence on the defendants but suspended all sentences except that for Ernst Mueller, president of the League.[27]

This so-called Siegfried case attracted considerable publicity. Editorials and reports in newspapers and national magazines condemned the Bund as a Nazi group and expressed no sympathy for the defendants. To Bundists the outcome was a "crying miscarriage of justice" and the defendants achieved martyrdom. Kuhn appealed for funds from local units and outside sympathizers to help defray legal expenses. Every court action directed at the Bund, no matter how insignificant or in which part of the country, would be fought with the resources of the organization's defense fund. At a public rally Kuhn announced that the Bund would appeal the case to a higher court, to the Supreme Court if necessary, and perhaps the "400,000 members of the organization" would be brought to the stand to testify that the Bund did not require an oath of allegiance to Hitler. On the weekend following the trial, about two thousand people gathered to picnic and watch parades at Camp Siegfried. During the affair 25,000 anti-Nazi leaflets were dropped on the camp from an airplane chartered by the Non-Sectarian Anti-Nazi League.[28]

The verdict in the Siegfried trial led Bundists to indulge in wishful thinking. They claimed that in Jewish circles a feeling of gaiety prevailed, while in Christian groups and among all fair-minded Americans there were expressions of indignation and disgust. At this Moscow show trial the "hidden hand" of Jews had held a firm grip over judge and jury. Jews really wanted to take over Camp Siegfried and rename it Camp Dickstein. This time they had gone too far in their harassment, because Jewish machinations embracing riots, arrests, investigations, invasions of meetings, and insulting propaganda were solidifying American opinion behind the Bund. As one Bundist explained, the time had come for a new attack on the opposition, for with unity and dedication "victory will be ours as it was for Adolf Hitler."[29]

NOTES

1. The *Times*, for example, extensively covered Bund affairs, and it provides a gauge to public interest in the movement. In 1936 the Bund received one entry in the *New York Times Index*, three columns in 1937, four columns of entries in both 1938 and 1939, two columns in 1940, and one in 1941.
2. Day, "American Opinion Toward National Socialism, 1933-1937."
3. *Weckruf*, February 4, 11, 1937; Ogden, *The Dies Committee*, pp. 41-42.
4. Bund Command No. 8, April 18, 1937; No. 11, July 28, 1937; *Weckruf*, August 12, 19, 26, 1937; Letter of Fritz Kuhn to whom it may concern, August 10, 1937, in RG 131, Box 142.
5. *Times*, June 17, July 17, 19, 22, 23, 25, 26, 27; August 2, 1937; *Weckruf*, July 29, August 5, 12, 19, 1937.
6. *Times*, August 19, 1937; Cook, *The FBI Nobody Knows*, pp. 232-233; *Weckruf*, September 2, 1937; Bund Command No. 13, September 14, 1937. Actually, the inner circles of the Roosevelt administration had been watching fascist activities for some time, as far back as 1934, and alerting the FBI to them. See Whitehead, *The FBI Story*, pp. 158-162.
7. *Times*, September 11, November 23, 24; December 6, 7, 10, 15, 1937; *Weckruf*, October 28, December 9, 16, 1937.
8. Transcript of the radio address delivered by Stefan Heym, in RG 131, Box 87.
9. *Times*, September 20, October 14, November 20, 24, 1937; *Weckruf*, November 25, December 9, 1937.
10. *Weckruf*, November 4, 11, 25; December 2, 9, 23, 1937; Bund Command No. 16, January 10, 1938.
11. *Times*, January 6, 14, 1938; *Weckruf*, January 20, 1938; Bund Command No. 17, February 17, 1938. Pressures from German officialdom also led Kuhn to change the Bund flag. In early January 1938 the German Ambassador in Washington, Hans Dieckhoff, sent a detailed dispatch to the Foreign Ministry requesting that Reich authorities avoid contacts with the Bund and discourage the organization from using the Nazi flag. Dieckhoff's suggestions were approved and apparently communicated to the Bund through the German consulate in New York. See Arthur Smith, *Deutschtum* pp. 99-100; Frye, *Nazi Germany*, pp. 86-87. On the Bund's activities and the decisions taken by Berlin see *Documents on German Foreign Policy*, Series D., Vol. 1.
12. Bund Command No. 17; *Weckruf*, January 20, 27; February 3, 10, 1938.
13. *Times*, February 8, 13, 14, 21; March 1, 1938; Dodd, *Ambassador Dodd's Diary*, p. 304; Remak, *"Friends of the New Germany,"*, p. 39; Arthur Smith, *Deutschtum*, pp. 92-102; Frye, pp. 85-87; Compton, *The Swastika and the Eagle*, pp. 63-68; Jonas, *Isolationism in America*, pp. 208-209. Dieckhoff informed Secretary of State Hull that Reich authorities ordered all German nationals out of the Bund and forbade the organization to use the Third Reich's emblem. He assured Hull that communications between the Bund and German agencies were banned. The Foreign Ministry did its utmost to maintain these edicts, but Fritz Kuhn's boastful and insincere pronouncements to Bund members and before public rallies about his control over German consulates and influence in German circles kept alive American suspicions that the Bund had intimate connections with Nazi agencies. A good analysis of Dieckhoff's role as German Ambassador to the United States is Warren F. Kimball, "Dieckhoff and America: A German View of German American Relations, 1937-1941."
14. *Times*, March 2, 1938; *Weckruf*, March 10, 1938; Frye, p.87
15. *Weckruf*, February 11, 25; March 25, April 8, May 6, 20; July 22, 29; September 23, October 14, 21; November 4, 25, 1937; January 20, 1938.
16. Jonas, pp. 209-210; Compton, p. 60.
17. *Weckruf* March 31, 1938; *Times*, March 26, April 4, 8, 9, 10, 11, 1938.
18. *Times*, April 21, 22, 23, 25, 28; May 4, 1938; *Weckruf*, April 28, May 5, 1938; "Imported Nazi Sadism."
19. *Weckruf*, May 5, 1938.

20. Bund Command No. 18, May 3, 1938.
21. *Times*, April 28, May 6, 7, 8, 10, 17, 18, 1938; *Weckruf*, May 12, 1938.
22. Ogden, pp. 32-34, 43-47; *Times*, May 27, 1938; Gellermann, *Martin Dies*, pp. 54-64; *Weckruf*, June 2, 16, 30, 1938.
23. Concern over the German-American Bund was only one of the many interests of the McNaboe Committee. For a general survey of the background, testimony, and results of the entire investigation, see Chamberlain, *Loyalty and Legislative Action: A Survey of Activity of the New York State Legislature, 1919-1949* and "New York: A Generation of Legislative Alarm" in Gellhorn, ed., *The States and Subversion*, pp. 242-245.
24. Letter of Fritz Kuhn to John J. McNaboe, June 15, 1938, in RG 131, Box 133; *Weckruf*, June 30, 1938; *Times*, June 23, 24, 25; July 1, 2, 1938. For the full testimony, see State of New York, *Report of Joint Legislative Committee*.
25. Seligmann, "The New Barbarian Invasion"; "Of Spies and Bund Men"; "Exposing the Bund's Home Ties"; "The Gestapo in the USA."
26. *Times*, May 30, 1938; *Weckruf*, June 16, 1938. Scrapbooks containing Schwinn's speech notes, photographs, and newspaper clippings of his West Coast activities are in RG 131, Boxes 5 and 6, labeled "Deutsches Haus, Inc." Deutches Haus was the name of the Bund's Western Gau headquarters in Los Angeles.
27. A complete transcript of the testimony, proceedings, and exhibits of the trial are in RG 131, Box 104; *Times*, July 7, 8, 12, 13, 1938.
28. *Times*, July 14, 1938; "The Yahoos of Yaphank"; "Uncle Sam's Nazis"; "Heiling Muffled"; *Weckruf*, July 21, 1938; Bund Command No. 19, July 12, 1938.
29. *Weckruf*, July 14, 21, 28; August 4, 11, 1938.

5

FREE AMERICA

The criticisms, attacks, violence, legal suits, and investigations directed at the American Nazi movement had an important consequence in that they led Bund leaders to develop an American-oriented program. It was anticipated that this program, formally adopted at the Bund's 1938 National Convention, would alter the organization's image as a Nazi annex and attract large numbers of Americans to the movement. The expected results never materialized, however. Hitler's menacing moves on the Continent, especially during the Sudeten crisis of September 1938, perturbed anti-Bund groups, and after the German Pogrom of November 1938 intense anti-Nazi sentiment developed in the German-American community. While these pressures on the organization swelled, Bundists pursued their new course with vigor and determination, heedless to the deepening and widening animosities directed at them.

On September 3, 1938, the Bund's most significant annual convention opened at the Turnhalle in New York with 632 delegates, representing units from coast to coast. Fritz Kuhn had insured a large gathering by alerting the local units to the "very great importance" of the convention and by pleading with unit leaders to make every sacrifice to participate in the occasion.[1] The convention was a closed affair for Bundists, lasting only three days; its sessions were complemented with mass rallies and celebrations in New York and at Camps Siegfried and Nordland.

Bundesführer Fritz Kuhn, Publicity Director G. Wilhelm Kunze, Eastern Gau Leader Rudolf Markmann, Midwestern Gau Leader George Froboese, and Western Gau Leader Herman Schwinn led the main discussions and issued new statements of policy, the delegates concurring in their views. The debates were astonishingly frank; no effort was made to conceal the problems the movement faced. Bundists expressed dismay over the intensity of the opposition and outlined the grave difficulties confronting them. Yet each report ended on a note of optimism and confidence, on a belief that, in spite of all the problems, the Bund would achieve greater success in the coming year. As usual, Bundists seemed to interpret the most discouraging events as evidences of progress and growth for their movement.

Of the problems facing the American Nazi movement, none perplexed Bundists more than their inability to attract significant German-American support. Their key aim had always been to bring all German-Americans into the National Socialist fold, yet by 1938 they could not boast of even partially fulfilling this goal. At the 1938 convention, after each Gau leader reiterated the coolness that many German-Americans expressed toward the Bund, Fritz Kuhn concluded that the organization had to choose between two alternatives: either it could accept the insults and attacks of hostile German-Americans or it could fight back with vehemence admitting no need for a change of policy. The enthusiastic applause given to the latter alternative led the Bundesführer to remark: "We shall go our own way without looking to either side—the way we have gone so far, straight ahead, and we shall let nothing swerve us from it."[2] In subsequent months Bundists began a campaign of vilification against any prominent German-American who criticized their movement, Hitler, or Nazi Germany.

Besides revealing the Bund's shallow comprehension of German-American indifference and antagonism to Nazism, the convention debates pointed to the organization's internal problems. These included the difficulty of attracting young members and teaching them the German language, the general membership's lack of interest in joining the OD, and the national leadership's inability to coordinate

Bund affiliates on the local level. Local officials of the three most important affiliates—the OD, the Youth Division, and the Prospective Citizens League—wanted national headquarters to allow them to determine their own policies—a demand which promoted jealousies, suspicions, and inefficiency.[3] In effect, the Bund's leadership principle was being questioned, but Kuhn was reluctant to take sides in organizational power struggles. This attitude fostered petty bickering which played havoc with the internal unity of the movement.

The economic condition of the Bund was one of the most important issues discussed at the 1938 convention. On this question the delegates gained some satisfaction. For the year from July 1937 to July 1938 the DKV had an income of $63,343.08 and a net profit of $920.41. The income from the AV Publishing Company, which printed the *Weckruf*, pamphlets, and leaflets for the same period, totaled $36,905.60, with a net profit of $341.91. Income from other sources—such as monthly membership dues, new membership fees, donations, admission to Bund events, and the sale of pins, insignia, and propaganda materials—was $14,733.94. Subtracting salaries, rent, travel allowances, telegrams, postage, and miscellaneous office expenses, there was a balance of $244.45. Although the organization was moving on an even financial keel, with membership dues providing enough income to maintain regular business, Bundesführer Kuhn correctly predicted that the greatest future threat to the movement would be financial. There were several potential financial problems. Propaganda and legal battles were expensive. Kuhn cited $700 for the cost of only one effort—distribution of his August 1937 Dickstein letter; the Bund had spent $10,000 on the Siegfried case. Another threat that provoked alarm was the growing number of members who were losing their jobs because of affiliation with the movement. If this number increased, a new fund would be needed to provide subsistence aid to unemployed Bundists. To help secure the Bund's economic future, Kuhn asked all members to cut costs, contribute to the legal defense fund, recruit new members, and win new subscribers to the *Weckruf*. Beyond these pleas, he outlined a plan for the creation of the National Adminstrative Properties Corporation, to be chartered at Wilmington, Delaware, which would bring all Bund properties, camps, DKV, and the newspaper under one administration. Each would continue as an individual enterprise but would be required to contribute at least 5 percent of its profits to the National Administrative Properties Corporation. Every Bund member would receive shares of the new corporation at a nominal fee. Kuhn predicted that this proposal, if implemented, would net a profit of $35,000 in its first year. The money would be used to fight court cases, establish travel bureaus and new camps, finance radio programs, buy factories, and create German communities. In short, the corporation would make the Bund completely self-sufficient and provide competition to the Jewish boycott of German goods. To the delegates this plan was "simply magnificent," and they voted unanimously to establish the new corporation.[4] But the National Administrative Properties Corporation never got beyond the planning stage; it may have been devised only to lift the morale of harassed Bundists. On the other hand, the Bund soon became so preoccupied with defending itself from outside attacks that it had no time to consider expansive plans.

Convinced of the justness and righteousness of their cause, Bundists assumed that the problems of economic security, internal cohesion, and German-American enmity toward their movement would resolve themselves in time. A new shift in ideology captured the delegates' paramount interest. Officially released to the press on the second day of the convention, it included an eight-point American program:

1. A socially just, white, Gentile-ruled United States.

2. Gentile-controlled labor unions free from Jewish Moscow-directed domination.

3. Gentiles in all positions of importance in government, national defense, and educational institutions.

4. Severance of diplomatic relations with Soviet Russia, outlawing of the Communist Party in the United States, prosecution of all known Communists for high treason.

5. Immediate cessation of the dumping of all political refugees on the shores of the United States.

6. Thorough cleaning of the Hollywood film industries of all alien, subversive doctrines.

7. Cessation of all abuse of the freedom of the pulpit, press, radio and stage.

8. A return of our Government to the policies of George Washington. Aloofness from foreign entanglements. Severance of all connections with the League of Nations.[5]

Adoption of this eight-point program did not mean that the Bund had forgotten its earlier stated aims of uniting German America under its wing and defending Germany and National Socialism. While pursuit of the old goals persisted, hereafter a greater effort would be devoted to recruiting Americans into the movement. This would be accomplished not only by publicizing a new program, but also by using a variety of other techniques. The delegates were told to use the term "white man" frequently and that the technique of bluffing was essential to success. Western Gau Leader Schwinn informed the convention: "We shall make the word 'Bluff' our motto. By this I mean that even if we do not control the German element, we shall nevertheless tell the politicans that we do."[6] Every opportunity would be seized to overstate the Bund's strength and influence. It was noted that some American newspapers set the movement's membership at the grossly inflated figure of 400,000. Although the Bund could count on only a few thousand members, there should be no attempt to correct the impression that the organization had enormous power over German America and was increasingly winning new adherents from the general American public. Along with these propaganda pointers, the delegates were advised to use English at rallies and in publications. Since many Bundists admitted that they had difficulty in reading German and argued that a large English section in the *Weckruf* would appeal to Americans, this change won general approval. The name of the paper was to be modified also, and the delegates agreed to submit suggestions for a new English title. To further this Americanization effort, Bundists were to seek alliances with right-wing societies. Kuhn contended that over two hundred native fascist organizations existed in the United States with aims similar to the Bund's. These groups were natural allies; it was in the movement's interests to promote their activities and literature as well as to attend their meetings.[7]

Continued debates on the Americanization of the Bund led some delegates to question the need for the Nazi salute. Investigations of the organization had drawn attention to it, and a few members claimed that their American friends sympathized with the movement but found the Nazi salute repulsive and alien. After a short debate Kuhn gave his decision:

> So long as I am at the head of the Bund the salute will remain . . . for two
> reasons: Every fascist organization in the entire world has the salute in some

form or other; it is the salute of the White Race . . . secondly, the salute is a symbol, . . . and it requires the courage of one's convictions to carry out this outward symbol.[8]

But he decided that the words "Free America" instead of "Sieg Heil" would be spoken when giving the salute. For most Bund events the "Bund Song," along with the "Star-Spangled Banner," would replace the "Horst Wessel Song," which would be sung only on special German occasions, when the swastika was fully displayed.[9]

On anti-Semitism, the ideological mainstay of the movement, the delegates saw no need for compromise. Indeed, the general thrust of the eight-point American program was a call for the establishment of a racial state similar to the Third Reich, with rigid restrictions placed on the ability of Jews to move into important power positions in American society. Bundists believed that this attack on Jews represented an unusual tactic. Anti-Communism, Gau Leader Schwinn argued, lacked a strong appeal because it was so widespread in American society. But, he continued, the Bund's anti-Communism which labeled Jews as the leaders of Communism caught the popular imagination:

> You can be convinced that 95% of the Americans agree with us that the Jew is a filthy scoundrel . . . .We must bring the attack on the Jews more in touch with politics, economics, and culture. I can assure you that you have a very agreeable theme in this battle. The frame of mind of the Americans is against the Jews. We must cut into this notch.[10]

Anti-Jewish pamphlets were to be promoted more vigorously, especially *The Protocols of the Wise Elders of Zion*. Hans Diebel, manager of the Aryan Book Store located at the Deutsches Haus in Los Angeles, claimed to have sold one thousand copies of this document in one year, and he felt that every unit could easily match his sales. Kuhn closed the sessions by thanking the delegates for their productive work and urging them to fight harder and never to doubt the national leadership.[11]

The 1938 convention represented the high water mark in the history of the Bund. Outwardly the organization appeared united, strong, and healthy. Kuhn and other leaders had formulated impressive plans to expand the movement. Their decision to discard some of the obvious Nazi features and move toward a more American orientation was expected to soften American public opinion. Yet the ideology of hate did not change; in fact, it became more repugnant.

And the debates at the convention had revealed tensions and jealousies within the movement which could only increase with time and under the pressures of hostile critics.

For several days after the convention, the Bund held mass rallies in New York, where officials of the movement gave bombastic, belligerent, and viciously anti-Semitic speeches. Each stressed that the Bund intended to fight the opposition with unrelenting intensity. A few suggested that efforts would be made to amend the U.S. Constitution so as to prohibit Jews from holding any appointive or elective public office on any level of government. Each called upon all Americans to join with the Bund to battle for a "Free America."[12] The new emphasis of the Bund on being "American" could not have been inaugurated with more insensitivity or arrogance.

Beginning in the fall of 1938, a series of sensational events, occurring in rapid succession, had a profound influence on the future of the American Nazi movement. First came the testimony of anti-Bund witnesses appearing before the Dies Committee. On September 29, in open hearings before the committee, one witness charged that Kuhn had made a secret pact of cooperation with German Ambassador Dieckhoff. The witness also believed that upon the Bundesführer's recommendation to Berlin authorities, any German official in the United States would be recalled. Dieckhoff quickly responded to this alarming testimony by informing the State Department that no understanding had ever existed between the Bund and himself or any other German diplomat. *Weckruf* editorials praised Dieckhoff's statement; they maintained that the Dies witnesses were "stooges" who spread lies and malicious gossip, as Willy Brandt had done in the Siegfried case.[13] Generally, the testimony given before the Dies Committee repeated accusations of previous investigations, and the Bund simply reiterated the customary denials. The coincidental timing of the hearings and the international crisis over Czechoslovakia, however, had the effect of sharpening anti-Bund sentiment to near-hysterical proportions.

For several months prior to the Munich Conference in late September 1938 the *Weckruf* had been interpreting the growing Czech crisis. With dull consistency it followed the Nazi propaganda line, concentrating on the single theme that the Sudeten Germans lived under oppressive conditions and that absorption of the Sudetenland into the Third Reich was the only reasonable solution to their plight.

The situation was compared to the American annexation of Texas and Great Britain's intervention in South Africa; in each case a foreign government murdered, terrorized, and discriminated against a minority of Americans or Englishmen seeking self-determination. Both America and Britain had acted wisely by forcibly annexing the areas to protect their subjects. The German Führer had hoped to resolve a similar situation in Czechoslovakia by peaceful negotiation, but his efforts were hampered by Jewish-controlled press agencies, which systematically tricked readers into believing that Germany was the aggressor. Bundists rejoiced when Hitler won his greatest diplomatic trimph at Munich. He was "the miracle man of the century," who returned the Sudetenland to its ancestral home and created a new and happier Europe, in which Germany stood firm against Bolshevism. Bundists regretfully noted that no American statesman had supported Germany as the champion of liberty. Instead, the Jews who controlled the administration agitated against the Reich by attributing new schemes of conquest to Hitler. The *Weckruf* carried articles by American anti-Semites which interpreted the Munich settlement as Hitler's victory over "Communist Jewry" and called for a federation of Nordic nations. The Munich agreement represented the first step toward fulfilling a pact which would insure cooperation among nations related by blood, preserve the purity of the white race, and prevent "monkeyhood from supplanting motherhood." In New York and at Camp Nordland mass rallies celebrating Hitler's triumph brought jubilant crowds to hear Kuhn and other Bund officials thank the German Chancellor for "liberating the Sudetens." At the Deutsches Haus in Los Angeles the local Bund ·unit held a mock burial of the Versailles Treaty.[14]

The Bund's elation over events in Europe was not shared by the Roosevelt administration, the American public, or American anti-Nazis. The administration was skeptical about the Munich accord, and the general public believed that Hitler had brought Europe to the brink of war. Incensed and alarmed over Hitler's success, anti-Nazis translated their anxiety and resentment into direct action against the Bund. They picketed Bund meetings in New York with banners that read: "Stop Hitler's Aggression" and "Return the Sudetenland to Czechoslovakia." In Union City, New Jersey, on October 2 a crowd of five thousand massed in front of a tavern where Fritz Kuhn intended to speak. Upon seeing Kuhn, the crowd yelled, "Kill him" and "Run him out of town" and showered the building with bricks. Local police persuaded the Bundesführer to cancel the meeting after some veterans burst into the tavern and began fighting with Bundists. A few days later, more than two thousand people milled outside a Bund rally in Syracuse, New York; despite a heavy police guard, they smashed windshields and slashed tires of cars belonging to Bundists. As the police escorted Bund members out of the building, cries of "Dirty Nazis" and "Why don't you go back to Hitler" came from the throng. At Oakland, California, the local Bund unit was ousted from its meeting hall because the owner felt that the members had become "especially cocky since Hitler went into Czechoslovakia." In Chicago, Bundists came to blows with anti-Nazis carrying pickets with the slogan "Save Czechoslovakia for Democracy." In Newark, New Jersey, a crowd laid seige to a Bund gathering; fist fights broke out when members tried to leave.[15]

The Bund did not relate these disturbances to the Czech affair but placed the responsibility on the Dies Committee. The false testimony of witnesses and the incendiary remarks of the committee members, Bundists argued, had inflamed public opinion and encouraged mob violence. Disregarding anti-Bund sentiment, they continued to implement the Americanization proposals of the September convention. On September 29, 1938, the Bund newspaper came out under the new title, *Deutscher Weckruf und Beobachter and the Free American*. A few days later, Fritz Kuhn issued orders to unit leaders calling for an aggressive recruitment campaign, with every member working to attract Americans into the movement through personal contacts and distribution of the Bund newspaper, pamphlets, and leaflets. He instructed larger units to hold a greater number of political meetings to draw an American audience. Each unit was to establish a bookstore to serve the American public. In line with this Americanization effort, the organization printed numerous pamphlets stating its new aims and purposes. Some carried advertisements which welcomed all "patriotic Aryan Americans" to Bund membership or urged them to attend Bund rallies and help save their country from Communism. Local units in New York City invited "white Americans" to evenings of friendship and understanding. The closing remarks on all such occasions urged the audience to join the Bund in the interests of a "Free America."[16] Bundists also attended meetings of right-wing organizations and distributed literature, such as William Pelley's anti-Semitic pamphlets and Father Coughlin's newspaper *Social Justice*. Although they never made strong contacts with native American fascist groups, Bundists praised the work of American anti-Semites and anyone else who espoused views similar to their own.

The next dramatic event affecting Bund fortunes came on November 7, 1938, when Herschel Grynszpan, a Polish Jew, shot and fatally wounded Ernst vom Rath, the German embassy's third secretary in Paris. This event precipitated the infamous "crystal-night pogroms," during which the Nazis systematically attacked Jewish life and property throughout Germany. Americans responded with shock and revulsion. President Roosevelt, stating that he did not believe such things could happen in the twentieth century, recalled the American ambassador from Berlin. Important leaders in every area of American life unanimously denounced Nazi barbarity. Before returning to Berlin, Hans Dieckhoff described the American public's rage and pointed out that even the most hardened anti-Semites sought to divorce themselves from the pogrom.[17]

Dieckhoff had overlooked the Bund; the *Weckruf* made no apologies for the Nazi cruelties. It compared them to attacks of anti-Nazis on Bund meetings and scoffed at American leaders and journalists who denounced the pogrom. A double standard seemed to exist: Americans wept over indignities inflicted on Jews in Germany, yet said nothing about the brutal treatment of Germans in Czechoslovakia, Poland, and Lithuania. Moreover, Bundists argued, every recent world crisis had resulted from the assassination of a prominent individual by Jews. This time the German government made the "international nation of parasites" pay for its crime by striking at all Jewish Communists within Germany. The Bund contended that ambassadors returning home would report the truth about the situation. Dieckhoff would note how Jews had whipped anti-German sentiment into a frenzy, and Ambassador Wilson would report to U.S. Secretary of State Cordell Hull that the matter was exaggerated and misrepresented.[18]

Influential segments of the German-American community did not follow the Bund in defending the Nazi pogrom. The Bund's open support of Hitler's policies sharpened the antagonisms between Kuhn's group and the Steuben Society of America, the most prestigious German-American organization. Theodore Hoffman, National Chairman of the Steuben Society, had been critical of the Friends of the New Germany but did not take a sharp anti-Nazi position until 1938, when he repudiated the Bund. Shortly after the November pogrom, the Steuben Society asked its members to approve a statement condemning Nazi persecution of Jews. The largest German-American newspaper, *New Yorker Staats-Zeitung und Herold*, viewed the pogrom as an example of the Nazi sadism which had disheartened Germans everywhere. In a panel discussion over New York's radio station WNYC, Victor Ridder, publisher of the *Staats-Zeitung*, Gustav W. M. Wieboldt, former New York Chairman of the Steuben Society, and Representative Hamilton Fish of New York denounced Hitler and the Bund. Wieboldt told the radio audience: "In my mind the Bund, together with Mr. Hitler, are nothing more than rats." The Bund interpreted these developments with contempt: Hoffman, Wieboldt, and the editors of the *Staats-Zeitung* were traitors to their race, who had shamefully surrendered themselves to Jews.[19]

In the weeks following the pogrom the dreary pattern of violence and vituperation between Bundists and anti-Bundists continued. The home of the Newark, New Jersey, Bund leader was stoned; pressures from anti-Nazi organizations forced the cancellations of Bund meetings in Nassau County, New York; some readers of the *Weckruf* cancelled their subscriptions. In a letter to the newspaper one German-American noted that he could not continue his subscription because he believed that recent stories of Nazi terror were true.[20]

These varied expressions of outrage did not deflect Bundists from staging a dramatic display of their new American program. Encouraged by the reversal of the Siegfried case decision by the Appellate Division of the Supreme Court of New York, Bundists made preparations for "a monster demonstration of true Americanism" to be held on February 20, 1939, at Madison Square Garden in honor of George Washington's Birthday. George Washington figured prominently in Bund literature as the father of American isolationism; a spectacular celebration commemorating his birthday, Bund leaders believed, would not only help identify the Bund as an American organization, but also contribute to their propaganda drive of keeping the United States out of European affairs.[21]

An extensive publicity campaign began in mid-November 1938, with full-page advertisements of the rally in the *Weckruf*. Handbills distributed on the streets of New York proclaimed:

Is America the coming Jewish Empire? Hear amazing facts that cannot be challenged on Monday, February 20, 1939, 8 P.M. at Madison Square Garden. . . . General Admission 40¢, reserved seats 75¢ and $1.00.[22]

At the DKV's annual German Exposition and Christmas Market, Bundists promoted announcements of the February 20 rally. Kuhn and his staff sent invitations to numerous congressmen and senators, right-wing leaders, veteran groups, prominent local officials, and civic organizations in New York City. Representative Martin Dies and New York State Senator John McNaboe were to be guests of honor. Instructions to local Bund units in the New York metropolitan area urged all members to sell tickets and speak to everyone about the affair. Kuhn wrote to Herman Schwinn and George Froboese, asking each Gau leader to deliver a twelve-minute speech at the rally and to make their remarks as sharp as possible. In an effort to attract a large turnout, the official rally program stressed the Bund's dedication to Americanism. The slogan "Free America" appeared frequently in advertisements and short articles. Americans were assured that the Bund's imitation of the Nazi salute was the universal salute of Aryans everywhere. Unlike the clenched fist of Communists, allegedly derived from an old Jewish custom, the Bund salute symbolized peace. A brief statement on the OD noted that its members carried no weapons and merely protected Bund gatherings from unruly lawless elements. The program listed the contributions of important German-Americans to American culture, from John Peter Zenger to Carl Schurz. Finally, Americans of Aryan descent were requested to support the Bund's cause by filling out the membership or sympathizer coupon.[23] The Bund's careful preparations were fulfilled; the rally received nationwide attention, becoming the most publicized of all of Kuhn's affairs.

The New York City administration took precautions to avoid incidents by cordoning off a two-block area around Madison Square Garden and assigning about two thousand policemen to positions inside and outside the huge sports hall. Despite these precautions, there was some trouble. Demonstrations by anti-Nazis, scuffles between Bundists and anti-Bundists, and telephone calls threatening to set off time bombs provided a tense atmosphere as three thousand OD men ushered approximately twenty thousand people to their seats. While the crowd waited for the beginning of the rally, a Bund band played marching songs. Banners with such slogans as "Wake Up

America—Smash Jewish Communism," "1,000,000 Bund Members by 1940," and "Stop Jewish Domination of Christian America," along with American and Bund flags decorated the Garden. A thirty-foot picture of George Washington hung behind the speaker's rostrum.[24]

The rally began with the massing of colors and Nazi standards on the floodlit stage. As the red-and-gold swastika standards passed down the aisles, many spectators stretched out their arms in the Nazi fashion. A spotlight played on the marching OD men. The hall rang with loud cheers when Bund National Secretary James Wheeler-Hill opened the assembly with the salutation, "My fellow Christian Americans." He charged the Roosevelt administration with disregarding George Washington's advice to avoid entangling alliances. The President's address of October 1937 and the attacks of cabinet members on German leaders and Germany pointed to a trend toward American involvement in European affairs, and Wheeler-Hill called upon the audience to dedicate itself to the Bund's task of restoring America to the principles expressed in George Washington's Farewell Address. Eastern Gau Leader Rudolf Markmann delivered a short speech attacking critics of the movement. Midwest Gau Leader George Froboese and Bund Publicity Director G. Wilhelm Kunze gave sardonic anti-Semitic addresses connecting the Roosevelt administration, labor unions, religious organizations, and press agencies with an international Jewish Communist conspiracy. References to "parasitical aliens," "Christ haters," "Jewish dadaists," and "the ever homeless parasite" helped to convey their message of hate. The final and longest speech was delivered by Fritz Kuhn. Using phrases such as "slimy conspirators" and "Jewish camarilla," Kuhn rambled through a curious discussion of American history, citing examples of alleged Jewish perfidy during the American Revolution, the Civil War, and the World War. He concluded by stating the program adopted at the 1938 Bund convention and urging Aryan Americans to join the Bund and help "Free America."[25]

Throughout the rally the crowd responded to the cues of the speakers with appropriate boos and cheers. Allusions to Harry Hopkins and Frances Perkins and to the President as "Frank D. Rosenfeld" brought loud boos and catcalls; references to Father Coughlin and the isolationist Senators Gerald P. Nye, Hiram Johnson, and William E. Borah elicited frenzied cheers and applause. Two incidents marred an otherwise orderly demonstration. When Rudolf Markmann spoke of the Golden Rule of the Aryan race, Dorothy Thompson, then a reporter for the New York *Herald Tribune*, burst into laughter. Police and OD men rushed to the press box and calmed the commotion. Later, as Kuhn approached the end of his speech, the crowd suddenly rose to its feet and roared with anger. A young man, Isidore Greenbaum, had broken through police lines, climbed onto the speakers' platform, and lunged at Kuhn. As Greenbaum shouted, "Down with Hitler," a dozen OD men grabbed him, threw him to the floor, and kicked and beat him. He was eventually rescued by the police, taken to court, and released the following day after paying a fine for disturbing the peace.[26]

The Madison Square Garden Rally produced a tremendous outburst of indignation. National magazines, such as *The Nation* and *The Christian Century*, detailed the affair to their readers, while *Life* devoted a photographic essay to the rally. More than any other single Bund event, it sparked editorial comment across the country. In Georgia, the Atlanta *Constitution* deplored the meeting; midwest newspapers including the Detroit *Free Press*, the Des Moines *Register*, and the Indianapolis *Star* called the event an insult to the memory of George Washington. A New York *Times* editorial expressed hope that the rally had startled New Yorkers and raised questions about the Bund's finances, private army, membership lists, and commitments to a foreign power. A survey of nationwide editorial opinion revealed a unanimous condemnation of the Bund's display of anti-Semitic propaganda but also a general belief that a ban on the meeting would have violated fundamental American civil liberties. Many editors made an excellent point by commenting that the best way to combat American National Socialism was to give it freedom to display its vulgar exhibitions. Besides galvanizing editorial comment, the Madison Square Garden affair sparked recriminations from veteran, civic, and fraternal organizations, especially in the New York metropolitan area. Here also newsreels of the Bund meeting were withdrawn from circulation because of the violent audience reaction. And a few days after February 20 two large anti-Bund rallies were staged. Anti-Nazi German-American organizations, such as the Federation of German-American Clubs and the German League for Culture, held a counter-George Washington Birthday Celebration in the Bronx for the purpose of demonstrating that not all German-Americans subscribed to Nazism. On March 3, 1939, a mass meeting, called "New York's answer to the Bund," was held at Carnegie Hall. The Speakers—including Mayor Fiorello LaGuardia, Dorothy Thompson, Dr. John Haynes Holmes of Community Church, and other prominent New Yorkers—assailed the Bund as an un-American, Nazi organization.[27]   The deep animosity felt by anti-Nazis found further expression in a number of letters to Fritz Kuhn threatening his life.

> Rat Fritz Kuhn,
>   You and the other rats better go back to Ratland or I will murder you in sight within one week. This is no idle threat. I am having you watched night and day. Better be a live rat under the Austrian rat in Ratland than a dead rat in the U.S.
>
> A   True   German[28]

The Bund interpreted the Madison Square Garden Rally as a demonstration of "unprecedented enthusiasm for Christian patriotic Americanism." The *Weckruf* magnified the disturbance caused by Greenbaum into an assassination attempt on the life of Fritz Kuhn. Occurring only a few weeks after the slaying of vom Rath in Paris, the Greenbaum incident provided another example of the workings of the worldwide Jewish conspiracy. This time, however, the murder attempt was foiled by the fists of brave OD men. Any effort to disparage the rally as an un-American demonstration represented an expression of Jewish sour grapes. Bundists casually dismissed the counter-celebration of anti-Nazi German Americans in the Bronx as a Communist gathering, while the Carnegie Hall meeting was a display of the fanaticism of Negroes, Jews, and Communists. The Bund had good reasons for believing that its monster demonstration was a great success. Letters of approval and congratulations from *Weckruf* readers filled the pages of the newspaper for weeks after the event. Most encouraging to Bundists was a profit of over $3,700 from the rally's proceedings.[29]

In Germany newspaper reports on the Bund meeting drew attention to the Greenbaum incident as an example of "Jewish terror in New York." Dr. Heinrich Borchers, German Consul General in New York, sent an accurate analysis of the event to the Foreign Ministry in Berlin. He admitted to being impressed by the Bund's ability to successfully organize a massive demonstration. While noting that the Bund made efforts to stress an American character, issued statements

Fritz Kuhn haranguing a Bund rally, 1938.

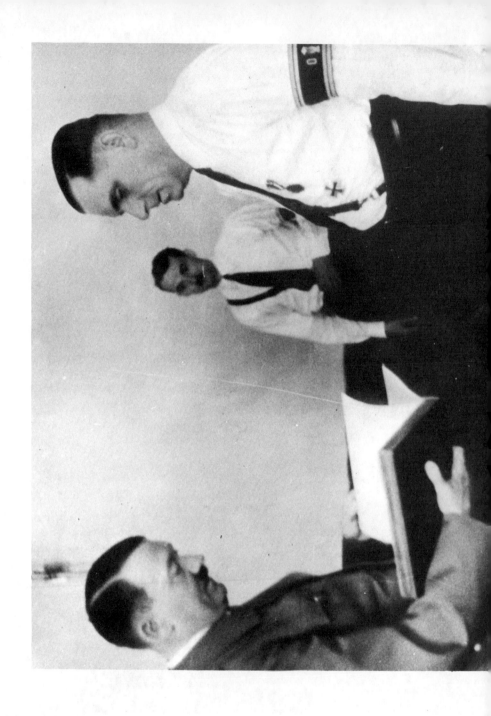

Kuhn presenting the *Golden Book of American Germandom* to Hitler, August 2, 1936.

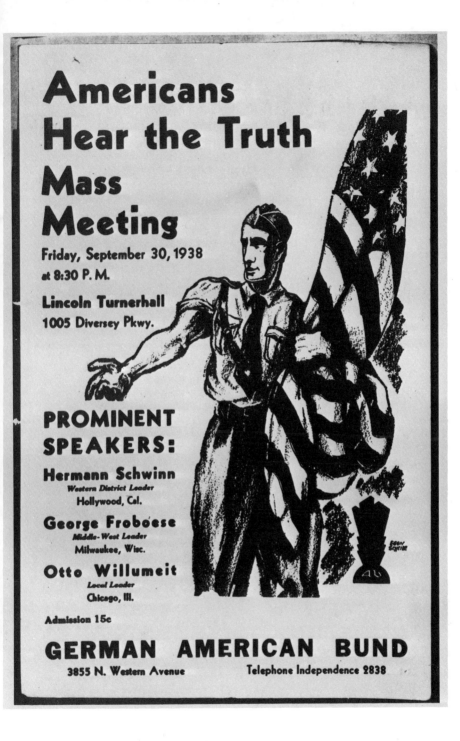

A Bund handbill, 1938.

Junges Volk

Zeitschrift der Jugendschaft des Amerikadeutschen Volksbundes

Jahrgang 5, Folge 2.   . Hornung (Februar) 1939.   Preis 10c.

German Blood Our Pride -
A Better America Our Goal!

ABRAHAM LINCOLN † 15. April 1865   HORST WESSEL † 23. Februar 1930

Beide starben für die Zukunft Ihres Volkes!

Magazine of the German-American Youth Division.

Bundists at a mass rally.

American Nazi Party magazine edited by George Lincoln Rockwell.

Rockwell (right) briefs some members of the American Nazi Party. Their "Hate Bus" is in the background. The bus had painted on it, in large red letters, "We Do Hate Race Mixing," "Lincoln Rockwell's Hate Bus," and "We Hate Jew Communism." (credit UPI Photo)

George Lincoln Rockwell, 1960 (credit UPI Photo).

opposing Nazism and fascism in the United States, and exercised some discretion by avoiding a flagrant display of the swastika, Borchers indicated that the rally nevertheless hurt German-American relations. The public's image of the Bund remained unchanged: Americans believed that it was a Nazi agency bent on destroying their nation by the Trojan horse method. The Consul General reported the public's intensely negative reaction to the rally—even Coughlin, in a radio address, had expressed his disapproval. In view of these circumstances, Borchers advised his superiors to dissociate themselves completely from Kuhn's movement. Reich interests could never be advanced by the Bund, he concluded, because of the organization's past mistakes, the rapid assimilation of immigrants into American life, and the dwindling influx of German migrants to the United States.[30]

Borcher's estimate of American sensitivity to the Nazi character of the Bund was demonstrated by the uproar over the February 20 rally. This public alarm showed the ineptness of the Bund leadership in coping with rising anti-Nazi sentiment. At its 1938 National Convention the Bund had made an effort to change its public image by dropping a few outward Nazi features and adopting what it believed to be an American program. In subsequent months it sought to attract Americans to the movement on the basis of these alterations. Yet, the Bund had not in fact, transformed itself enough either to win the support of large numbers of Americans or to modify anti-Nazi public opinion. Bundists nevertheless did not grow tired of putting their new program before the public, and in the spring of 1939 they began a spirited propaganda drive. Pro-American rallies featured speakers who talked about "Jewish Democracy in Action" while crowds hissed and laughed at Jews and Communists. Kuhn went on a nationwide tour of major units during which he promised that huge rallies similar to the Madison Square Garden affair would soon be held throughout the country.[31] The Bundesführer ordered local units to hold more celebrations and organize new recruitment drives until one hundred million people were organized into an Aryan political movement.

Bund members, recruit sympathizers! The language they speak, or the country to which they belong is of no concern. . . . The circle must grow, and quickly, not only for the good of any group of people, not for the good alone of our American nation, but for the preservation of the Aryan race and its state and its culture.[32]

This campaign extended even to the American Indian community, where a few individuals, bitter over lost treaty rights, were attracted to the Bund's anti-Semitism. Racial mythologists in the Third Reich had long identified American Indians as well as Japanese as true Aryans. Taking the position that Nazism respected Indian rights, the Bund distributed its literature to Indian sympathizers and featured two Indian chiefs as speakers at rallies. A Cherokee, Chief New Moon, who spoke at Camp Nordland, identified himself as "a full-fledged Nazi" and called for a Nazi-Indian entente against Communism. Elwood A. Towner, an Oregon attorney connected with the Siletz Reservation, took the name Chief Red Cloud and addressed numerous Bund gatherings on the West Coast, in New York City, and at Nordland. Towner gave a dramatic show. Appearing in full Indian dress decorated with swastikas, he discussed the Indian origins of the swastika and the need for cooperation between Indians and Germans against Jews, whom he referred to as *chuck-na-gin*, an Indian name meaning children of Satan and gold worshipers. Such displays led Oregon Indian groups to repudiate Towner and the Bund. The Commissioner of the Indian Bureau, John Collier, aware of Bund activity among the Indians, worked vigorously to combat it. For this effort he took heavy verbal abuse particularly from Herman Schwinn, who called him "Red Johnny" and repeatedly demanded his dismissal. [33] Fritz Kuhn placed the Bund's work among the Indians into a broader framework. In an interview with a reporter from *Ken*, Kuhn predicted a general American uprising within one year. The Bund would not launch this revolution, he argued, but the injustices inflicted by Jews upon Indians as well as all Americans was preparing the way for such an event.[34]

Kuhn and other Bund leaders sincerely believed that their program calling for a "Free America" was receiving tremendous support and awakening the people. They were partially right. By the spring of 1939 news about the Bund was familiar to most Americans. The country was indeed waking up to the American National Socialist movement, but not in a manner described and wished for by Fritz Kuhn. The more intensely he promoted Nazism, the more virulent became the public's repulsion from it.

NOTES

1. Bund Command No. 19, July 12, 1938; No. 20, August 16, 1938.
2. *Minutes of the 1938 National Convention of the German-American Bund,* p. 36. The author wishes to thank Mr. J. Walter Yeagley, U.S. Assistant Attorney General, for providing him with a zeroxed copy of this document (hereafter cited as *Minutes.*)
3. *Minutes,* pp. 88-89, 98-109.
4. *Minutes* pp. 12-19, 43, 121-133. A few documents indicating the purpose and scope of the National Properties Administration Corporation are in RG 131, Box 192.
5. *Minutes,* p. 66.
6. *Minutes,* p. 71.
7. *Minutes,* pp. 47-62, 70-81, 88-98.
8. *Minutes,* pp. 84-85.
9. *Minutes,* pp. 84-87. The words of the Bund song are: "For liberty and truth we fight/ With words and deeds and song./ For honesty and human right/ We stand, and not for wrong./ All true friends of New Germany,/ And this with pride we say,/ Are Friends of Peace, will always be/ Friends of the U.S.A."
10. *Minutes,* p. 88.
11. *Minutes,* pp. 133-146. The Aryan Book Store sold such items as Elizabeth Dilling, *The Red Network*; Adolf Hitler, *Mein Kampf*; W. D. Pelley, *Jews in our Government, The Jewish Question, Communism's Iron Grip on the CIO*; and notoriously anti-Semitic pamphlets including *An Analysis of Zionism, The Hidden Hand of Judah, The Protocols of the Wise Elders of Zion,* and *Thus Speaks the Talmud.* The bookstore advertised its wares under the slogan, "World Jewry wants war to strengthen their supremacy." See RG 131, Box 9, labeled "Deutscher Haus, Inc.," for book and pamphlet lists. The Bund also operated the Germania Bookstore, located near its national headquarters in the Yorkville section of New York. It distributed Bund literature, sold tickets to meetings, and carried a large assortment of anti-Semitic propaganda.
12. Broadsides announcing the rallies, in RG 131, Box 193. Speeches delivered, in *Weckruf,* September 8, 15, 1938.
13. *Times,* August 13, 19; September 29, 30; October 1, 1938; "The War on Isms"; *Contemporary Jewish Record,* I, pp. 70-71; Ogden, *The Dies Committee,* pp. 51-52, 57-73, 86-88; *Weckruf,* August 18, 25; September 1, October 6, 20, 1938.
14. *Weckruf,* October 6, 13, 27, 1938; *Times,* October 3, 1938; RG 131, Box 6, labeled "Deutsches Haus, Inc.," contains American newspaper clippings of the West Coast Bund celebration of the Munich settlement.
15. Jonas, *Isolationism in America,* p. 210; Compton, *The Swastika and the Eagle,* p. 60; *Times,* October 2, 3, 16, 17, 27, 1938; *Contemporary Jewish Record,* I, pp. 72-73.
16. Bund Command No. 21, October 8, 1938; Bund leaflets and pamphlets stating the aims and purposes of the Bund, in RG 131, Boxes 1 and 20; *Weckruf,* September 29, November 3, 1938; *Times,* October 31, 1938.
17. "The Nazi Pogroms: Digest of Public Opinion"; Compton, p. 57.
18. *Weckruf,* November 17, 24, 1938.
19. *Times,* October 3, 9; November 23, 1938; *Statement of the National Council of the Steuben Society of America,* November 21, 1938, in RG 131, Box 142; *Weckruf,* November 24, December 8, 1938.
20. "Nazi Plague Infects City"; *Times,* November 13, 14, 17, 19, 20, 22, 29; December 3, 5, 15, 1938; Anonymous letters from subscribers to the Bund newspaper, in RG 131, Box 137.
21. *Times,* November 5, 1938; *Weckruf,* November 10, 1938.
22. Bund handbill, in RG 131, Box 88.
23. Bund leaflets announcing the Madison Square Garden Rally, in RG 131, Boxes 116 and 140; *Official Program and Guide to the German Exposition and Christmas Market,* December 15-23, 1938; Invitational form letters of Fritz Kuhn to Martin Dies, John McNaboe, and other individuals and organizations; Letter of Fritz Kuhn to all members;

Letter of Fritz Kuhn to George Froboese, Herman Schwinn, in RG 131, Box 140; *Mass Demonstration For True Americanism,* Official Bund program, in RG 131, Box 101.

24. *Times,* February 21, 1939.
25. *Six Addresses Delivered At Madison Square Garden,* New York, 1939, in RG 131, Box 140.
26. Alson Smith, "I Went to a Nazi Rally"; "Hessian Day Rally"; "New York Nazis Beat Up a Jew at Bund Meeting."
27. "The German-American Bund Meeting"; "The Nazis are Here"; Britt, "Poison in the Melting Pot"; *Times,* February 21, 22, 23, 24, 25, 27; March 1, 4, 1939.
28. Anonymous letter to Fritz Kuhn, March 9, 1939, in RG 131, Box 194.
29. For an itemized financial account of the Madison Square Garden Rally, see RG 131, Box 140.
30. *Times,* February 22, 26, 1939; *Documents on German Foreign Policy,* Series D. Vol. IV, pp. 675-678.
31. Broadsides announcing pro-American rallies, in RG 131, Box 19; *Weckruf,* May 11, 1939.
32. Bund Command No. 22, June 1, 1939.
33. National Archives, *Record Group 75;* for a brief contemporary account, see "Red Indians in Brown Shirts."
34. Oliver, "Fritz Kuhn Verbatim."

6

THE END
OF THE BUND

Between 1939 and 1941 the German-American Bund fell apart for a variety of reasons. Public revulsion against the February 20 rally provided the impetus for galvanizing the New York City administration, through the joint efforts of Mayor LaGuardia and District Attorney Thomas E. Dewey, into investigating Bund finances. In March and April 1939 Commissioner of Investigation William B. Herlands conducted an inquiry to determine if the Bund had evaded paying local sales and business taxes. In early May agents of the District Attorney seized documents from Bund national headquarters relating to the organization's corporation. On the basis of evidence collected from these sources, the New York County Grand Jury charged Fritz Kuhn with stealing $14,548 of Bund money; he pleaded not guilty and was released on $5,000 bail.[1]

Instead of facing this challenge with prudence and self-control, the Bund began a campaign of vilification and innuendo against Dewey. Articles and editorials in the *Weckruf* reeked with threats and violence. Kuhn issued a public statement maligning the District Attorney. The organization's 1939 convention produced resolutions deriding New York City justice and authorizing Kuhn to take any means and use any or all of the Bund's financial resources to defend himself and the movement. In late September, Dewey raised the bail of the May indictment to $50,000 on the ground that Kuhn planned to leave the court's jurisdiction. Unable to raise this amount immediately, Kuhn spent several days in jail while his followers intensified their mudslinging. Leaflets filled with anti-Semitic references were distributed on the streets to solicit funds for Kuhn's defense; no exaggeration was too extreme. Nor did Kuhn himself act with restraint on other matters demanding a display of moderation. His dramatic appearances before the Dies Committee in Washington were characterized by quarreling, bickering, angry shouting, and incoherent testimony. As the pressures upon him increased, his behavior became more aggressive and paranoiac: he saw himself encircled by enemies determined to destroy him.[2]

Fritz Kuhn's trial opened in New York on November 9, 1939, amid wide publicity. The press noted that the date was the sixteenth anniversary of Hitler's Beer Hall Putsch in Munich. During the three weeks of the trial Kuhn's attorney, Peter L. F. Sabbatino, gave a stormy performance, not allowing one session to pass without protesting what he alleged to be a mistrial. Sabbatino attempted to show that since the basic organizational pattern of the Bund, the Führerprinzip, gave the Bundesführer total freedom over the organization's funds, he could not be charged with larceny. Defense witnesses supported this contention, referring to the organization as "a one-man Bund" and asserting that Kuhn even had the right to throw Bund funds "down the sewer." The chief prosecutor, Assistant District Attorney Herman J. McCarthy, challenged Sabbatino's interpretation of the Führerprinzip; he claimed that it did not give Kuhn such wide authority. When Sabbatino produced a resolution adopted at the 1939 Bund convention which gave Kuhn absolute power over the organization, McCarthy noted that it was made after the Bundesführer had come under indictment. A further snag in the defense attorney's argument occurred during the cross-examination of Bundist Gustav J. Elmer, who confessed that Kuhn could spend Bund money on anything except women. Unfortunately for Kuhn, subsequent testimony revealed that he had spent the organization's money on that very item: he had paid $717 for moving the furniture of a Mrs. Florence Camp, and $60 for a doctor bill of a Mrs. Virginia Cogswell, a former Miss America, at a New York hotel. The intimate nature of the relationship between Kuhn and Mrs. Camp was disclosed when his telegrams and letters to her were read in court. Closing lines read: "Great love and kisses. All my thoughts with you,

love you, my everything. Fritzi." Along with this embarrassing testimony, accountants from the district attorney's office exposed the
fact that Kuhn had not deposited large sums of money into the
Bund's bank account in the fall of 1938 as he had claimed, and a
lawyer employed by Kuhn charged that the Bundesführer owed him
several thousands of dollars for legal services. The inference was that
Kuhn had used the money collected from units for the Siegfried case
for his personal pleasure. While constantly pointing to the Führerprinzip in his effort to clear Kuhn, Sabbatino developed another line
of defense; he charged Dewey with having anti-Bund motives for
prosecuting Kuhn. To support this cry of persecution, Dewey was
called to the stand and asked if he had "personal animus" against the
Bundesführer. Dewey frankly admitted that he viewed the Bund with
contempt and the defendant "as a nuisance to the community;" he
added, however, that his personal opinions had nothing to do with
the case. In the end the defense succeeded in eliminating five of the
original twelve indictments for lack of sufficient evidence, and the
case rested on Kuhn's alleged misuse of $1,217 of Bund funds. This
included the money he had advanced to Mrs. Camp and his theft of a
$500 Bund legal payment. The judge instructed the jury to decide if
the Führerprinzip had any validity on the Camp transaction, while
on the question of the lawyer's fee conflicting testimony confused
the issue. Kuhn swore that he had paid the fee; the lawyer claimed
that he had received no payment. But the prosecution presented
documents which apparently proved that Kuhn had forged a $500
entry in a Bund account book. The judge told the twelve jurors that
if they viewed this as evidence to conceal larceny, Kuhn should be
judged guilty of forgery. After eight and a half hours of deliberation,
the jury found Kuhn guilty of both larceny and forgery. On December 5 he left New York for Sing Sing, to begin a prison sentence of
two and a half to five years.[3]

The imprisonment of Fritz Kuhn had a twofold significance for
the future of the German-American Bund. For one, it alerted Reich
authorities, especially the DAI, into finally recognizing the futility of
the Bund's cause, a conclusion the German Foreign Ministry had
reached long before Kuhn's incarceration. Devoted to promoting a
National Socialist Deutschtum among Germans abroad, the DAI was
the most important propaganda and information-gathering agency
which maintained correspondence with the Bund. From Stuttgart,

Germany, it sent propaganda and reports on worldwide Deutschtum activities, promoted Bund visits to the Reich, and kept an extensive file on the American National Socialist movement. The information it received through newsclippings and personal correspondence was usually distorted to show that the Bund represented a vigorous and growing Nazi element. This uncritical judgment, along with the fact that some DAI officials were ex-Bundists—Walter Kappe, former editor of the *Weckruf*, and Fritz Gissibl, former leader of the Friends of the New Germany—led the Stuttgart agency to discount American anti-Nazi feeling and to support the Bund at a time when its appeal and strength were actually diminishing. Throughout 1939, however, Kuhn's legal difficulties aroused apprehension and encouraged a more critical evaluation of American Nazism, and after receiving a report through the Foreign Ministry from Consul General Borchers analyzing the negative effects of the Bundesführer's trial, the DAI severed relations with the Bund. There were others in Germany who refused to face reality. Kameradschaft USA, an organization of ex-Bundists who had returned to Germany, kept records of its members' American experiences, held nostalgic meetings, and worked to win support for the Bund. Its small numbers, as well as the outbreak of war, made this group's efforts inconsequential.[4] In short, the action of the DAI cut the Bund off from this important agency and meant that hereafter communications with the Reich could only be erratic and surreptitious.

Kuhn's imprisonment also had a disastrous effect on the Bund's internal unity. The bitter strife that developed proved to be one of the movement's greatest maladies. Initially, in the weeks following Kuhn's trial, the Bund appeared to be united behind its imprisoned leader. The *Weckruf* emphasized his innocence, asserting that he was a victim of a Jewish plot. The new Bundesführer, G. Wilhelm Kunze, a native American, issued a public statement praising Kuhn's past management of the organization and charging that the "so-called conviction of Fritz Kuhn" was a travesty of justice. Kunze sent a Christmas greeting to Kuhn pledging his "unshaken loyalty" to the former Bundesführer. A New Year's proclamation referred to the conviction as "a crucifixion" and announced that the Bund would continue fighting for a Christian America and a "free Kuhn." The youth magazine *Junges Volk* published articles exonerating Kuhn, a victim of Jewish revenge. This entire display of unity, however, was a façade. On December 6, 1939, the day after Kuhn went to prison, the Bund's executive committee met in special session at national headquarters to depose Fritz Kuhn from office and to expel him from Bund membership. His past actions were called "dishonorable and disgraceful." G. Wilhelm Kunze was officially elected the new Bundesführer.[5]

The committee's repudiation of Kuhn was never formally communicated to the membership. Instead, Kunze moved to clamp his authority over the organization by concentrating on internal security, threatening expulsion to any member who violated his instructions. His new orders forbade members to give information to journalists, send letters to government agencies, or make public remarks about political events. Although members could cooperate with other organizations having similar rightist aims, they were forbidden to join any other group unless national headquarters granted written permission. Under the new leader, entrance to full Bund membership would be granted only after a six-month investigation of each prospective member, and all citizens of foreign countries would be screened out of the movement. Kunze believed that criticism would lessen if every unit staged fewer political meetings and more singing and athletic events, although unit celebrations of George Washington's birthday as well as Hitler's would continue, privately if necessary. To further internal cohesion, and also to clear up the confusion created at Kuhn's trial over the leadership principle, he abrogated the Bund constitution and issued a new set of rules and regulations which placed greater emphasis on the powers of the national leader. To each member the Bundesführer represented the supreme law, and he rendered the final decisions on every matter concerning the movement.[6]

Kunze encountered difficulties in asserting his authority. He never won the respect and obedience of the entire membership. Members were required to follow the Bundesführer without question, but many refused even to recognize Kunze as national leader. Others ignored his orders. This situation, amounting to a crisis of confidence, resulted from a split between pro and anti-Kuhn factions within the units. While the larger anti-Kuhn element supported Kunze, its adherents demanded a greater voice in determining the choices and power of the leadership. They believed that Kuhn had possessed too much power and had used it carelessly, in ways harmful to the movement's interests. By stressing this point to Kunze, they hoped to prevent him from exercising arbitrary authority. The smaller pro-Kuhn faction had an even more divisive effect on the Bund. This group was most uncooperative, constantly fomenting dissent with bits of gossip and innuendoes about the leadership. Bitter over the Bund's failure to appeal her husband's case, Mrs. Kuhn became its rallying point. She herself wrote letters to all units in which she denounced the new leaders as scoundrels. Soon the organization was splintered into quarreling, schismatic groups with rival factions fighting comically at times for control over meeting halls. Opposing groups brawled, stole each others' keys, changed locks, and engaged in midnight break-ins to capture unit funds and documents.

A more serious contention forced the closing of Camp Siegfried. A clique of members, chiefly from the Brooklyn unit, refused to recognize Kunze as national leader and viewed Siegfried as their own property. When the executive committee tried to reorganize the camp on a sounder legal and financial basis, these dissidents withheld legal documents and Bund money. Along with the fact that the camp was deeply in debt, this problem led Kunze to close Siegfried, ordering members to sever all ties with it.[7]

All the internal strife was aggravated by financial debts and confusion. Kuhn's trial had cost the organization $13,000, and no contributions were offered to offset this loss. Kunze saw the lack of funds as the greatest problem facing the Bund, and in almost every Command he pleaded for money. In an effort to pay for various legal proceedings and to make the Bund financially solvent, he tried several remedies: he ordered half the cash on hand in each unit to be sent to his New York office. In addition to assessing a minimum contribution of one dollar per member for a new reconstruction fund he required a monthly fee of one dollar for every male member and sixty cents for every female member for national headquarters. In addition, members were asked to buy a new Bund pin as a symbol of honor and sacrifice. The pin cost ten dollars for married men, five dollars for married women, and twelve dollars for a single person. Moreover, every Bundist had the obligation to sell ten dollars worth of nonvoting shares in the AV Publishing Company as well as extra copies of the Bund newspaper. These requests failed to yield significant results: members chafed at increased financial demands and

simply refused to send money to national headquarters. Their depleted numbers compounded the problem. By August 1940 membership had dropped to two thousand—an interesting figure, showing the
extent to which the movement had disintegrated. The difficulty of
obtaining funds was complicated by the fact that Kuhn had kept no
records of his business transactions. This negligence created legal
problems, for in the absence of records, law-enforcement agencies
and tax officers in New York and elsewhere were threatening Bund
officials with penalty taxes and jail sentences for deliquency. When
Bundists sought legal assistance to handle these and other cases, they
found themselves charged excessive fees. Their lawyers candidly
admitted and defended this practice, explaining that in aiding Bundists they faced ostracism and lost clients and therefore had to make
up losses by tripling fees on Bund cases.[8]

Although the Bund was close to total disintegration as a movement, it was still capable of exciting public interest and anxiety by
its persistent display of belligerent propaganda. Soon after Germany
invaded Poland in September 1939, the Bund published a statement
which defended the Nazi-Soviet Non-Aggression Pact, demanded
strict observance of American neutrality, and announced its sympathy with the German war effort. Units were instructed to stress the
theme of neutrality in handbills and at public meetings; members and
sympathizers were told to contact legislators with a demand for
American isolation from the war; and rallies were advertised as
protests against "war-mongering British propaganda." All these
points were repeated in the Bund newspaper. Under its new abbrevia-
ted title, *The Free American*, the editorial page of every issue carried
a short statement telling Americans to remember that Britain had
forced the war on Germany. After France fell in late June 1940,
numerous articles noted that Germany looked beyond this glorious
victory by seeking a new rapprochement with the Vichy regime. But
more important, the pieces commented, German victories ended
British domination of the Continent and inaugurated a century of
peace. In these analyses the Bund reflected the Nazi propaganda line.
German propaganda sources, such as Transocean Service and the
German Library of Information in New York, dwelled on anti-British
themes, and the Bund readily utilized their publications.[9]

Every move of the Roosevelt administration which appeared to
increase American commitment to Britain received bitter criticism

from the Bund. Under-Secretary of State Summer Welles' mission to Europe to confer with the heads of the British, French, Italian, and German governments in February 1940 was compared to missions undertaken by Colonel House, Woodrow Wilson's adviser, on the eve of America's entrance into World War I. Welles, it was claimed, was, like House, an Anglophile, who hoped to discover Hitler's plans and reveal them to the British. The whole affair represented a British and possibly a Jewish plot to drag the United States into the war. Congressional approval of funds for preparedness activities and the destroyer-base deal were described as examples of the administration's squandering of the people's money and property. According to the *Free American*, the first peacetime draft law in American history, passed in September 1940, showed that Roosevelt intended to solve the country's unemployment problem by sending Americans to Europe to die for England. A provision of the conscription law barring Bund members from employment in vital industries brought indignant protests from Kunze, and he ordered all Bundists to refuse induction into military service.[10]

Roosevelt's obvious support for Britain led the Bund to work against his reelection in 1940. It warned that a third term for the Democrats would lead to dictatorship and put American boys into European trenches. The Republicans under Wendell Willkie offered the best hope for America, yet the Bund avoided giving him a blanket endorsement, adopting the slogan, "Don't throw your vote away, but don't vote for Roosevelt." The fact that Willkie could claim German descent pleased Bundists, but they correctly noted that his ancestry had generated a whispering campaign which stigmatized him as a Nazi. In the week before election day the Bund's cry that a Roosevelt victory meant war became more shrill, and the *Free American* predicted that German-Americans, disgusted with FDR's pro-British policies, would vote in a solid bloc for Willkie. With Roosevelt's reelection the Bund at first attributed Willkie's defeat to his support of New Deal policies and of American aid to Britain. Later, when the Republican candidate became an active interventionist and supported the Lend-Lease Act, the Bund became enraged. Kunze published an open letter to Willkie in which he denounced him with "utter revulsion." "Mr. Willicke-Willkie" was "a political stooge of international financiers" who had Jewish rather than German ancestry.[11]

Throughout 1940 and 1941 the Bund participated in the intense foreign-policy debate between interventionists and isolationists. Kunze ordered members to encourage the activities of every isolationist senator and congressman through personal letters and telegrams, making no reference to the Bund. Congressmen would be impressed, he believed, by a flood of several hundred letters coming from individuals in all parts of the country. The *Free American* publicized non-Bund antiwar rallies and carried the speeches and articles of isolationist senators and newspapers. It joined Elizabeth Dilling and protesting mothers' groups in an emotional debate on the Lend-Lease Act. The passage of this "dictator bill" became the "great American tragedy," a victory for financiers, British propagandists, and Jews. Americans were urged to join and to support such isolationist organizations as the America First Committee. The *Free American*'s endorsement of America First caught the attention of John T. Flynn, Chairman of the Committee's New York chapter, who promptly repudiated the Bund's patronage. Charles Lindbergh's fervent isolationist activities brought admiring comments from Bundists. He exemplified the "finest qualities of old-time Americanism" and courageously demanded that the country mind its own business. Excerpts from Lindbergh's speeches received front-page coverage in the Bund newspaper, where attention was drawn to his arguments that the United States could not be invaded nor could she win the war for England. On the other hand, William Allen White and the Committee to Defend America by Aiding the Allies took stinging criticism. Bundists joined the chorus of isolationist committees in charging that White's committee was financed by international bankers and munitions makers.[12]

While stressing the need for American neutrality, the *Free American* printed accounts glorifying Hitler's conquests in Europe. News stories stressed the effectiveness of German U-boat attacks on British shipping, British atrocities, the warm relationships between Germany and the occupied countries, the high morale of the German people, and Hitler's genius for military strategy. In the spring of 1941, when Hitler's armies stormed into the Balkans, Bundists called the campaign a defensive measure against British intrigue in Yugoslavia and Greece. Nazi soldiers had driven back the anti-German forces in a rout worse than Dunkirk. To Bundists the war was a battle of freedom for the German people and National Socialism. It transcended national boundaries and became a great world struggle between the forces of decadent Jewish democracy and the armies of progressive National Socialism.

The acclamation of Hitler's conquests proved most damaging to the Bund. Opinion polls showed that the majority of Americans favored aid to Britain and viewed Hitler and Nazism with contempt. Many allowed their opinions to turn into fear over real and imagined fifth-column activities. To these people Hitler's lightning victories seemed intelligible only by attributing them to some mysterious, undermining power of an international fifth column. In 1940 reports from citizens to the FBI on suspected fifth-column activities averaged 2,800 a day. Many newspapers and popular magazines, as well as the President in his fireside chats, pointed to the unsuspected treachery of aliens, traitors, spies, and saboteurs. Since the Bund harbored aliens and defended Nazi conquests, it became suspect and was subjected to a series of annoyances. Law-enforcement officers near Camp Nordland kept lists of car licenses of people visiting the camp and sent them to the FBI. In mid-September 1940 an explosion at the Hercules Powder Plant in New Jersey raised the cry of sabotage, and FBI agents questioned Bundists at Nordland. A New Jersey sheriff raided the camp in the hope of finding hidden arms and ammunition, presumably taken from the Hercules Company. A search by local authorities of the Bund's Chicago headquarters, seeking evidence to support an Illinois tax suit against the organization, produced a list of Bundists allegedly serving in the American military. The charge led to another FBI investigation. The simmering concern over a secret war against America found further expression in Congress. Federal appropriation acts excluded Bundists from employment, including work on the WPA. Senator Robert LaFollette attached a provision to an unsuccessful Fair Labor Practices Bill which kept Communists and Bundists from employment in interstate and foreign commerce. Two laws passed in 1940 showed interest in alien activities and established surveillance over Communists and Bundists. The Foreign Agents Registration Act required all aliens to register with the federal government, and the Voorhis Act required registration with the Justice Department of all organizations whose aim was the overthrow of a government by violence and whose political activities where subject to foreign control.[13]

In facing these new onslaughts, the Bund took but one line of defense. Any act or legislation directed against it was interpreted as an example of anti-German hysteria similar to measures directed at German-Americans during World War I. The raids on Nordland and on the Chicago Bund headquarters, the order barring Bundists from the WPA, the anti-Bund provisions of the appropriation acts, all proved that history repeated itself: just as in 1917 and 1918, German-Americans were caught in a reign of terror. It is significant that in editorializing on this position the Bund newspaper toned down its anti-Semitism, and its anti-Communism lacked the fervor of earlier years. Now most anti-Semitic articles in the *Free American* were printed in German.

This restraint did not apply to Nazi activities at Nordland in the spring of 1940. Speakers at camp rallies praised Hitler for freeing Europe of "Jewish czars," charged that Roosevelt and his "Jewish bosses" represented the real fifth column, and boasted that the Bund would rid the country of Jews and free America. Anti-Bund reaction was swift: four Bundists were indicted under a 1935 New Jersey race-hatred law for making these anti-Semitic statements. In mid-August 1940 a joint Ku Klux Klan and Bund gathering at Nordland brought an extremely hostile press reaction. The Bund advertised the affair as an antiwar, pro-American rally, and while Bundists attacked Jews, Klansmen struck at Catholics. Speakers pointed to the similarities between the principles of the Bund and the Klan. The press gave thorough coverage to a scuffle at the rally between Kunze's OD and a pro-Kuhn group which distributed leaflets for Kuhn's appeal.[14]

An appeal to members to become more fervent in their service to National Socialism became the main theme of the Bund's annual convention which opened in Chicago on August 31, 1940. A mere thirty-eight delegates attended the secret two-day affair. Most of them reported that "insane persecutions" had caused some members to drift away; while others, fearing harassment from anti-Nazis, refused to attend meetings. Kunze told the delegates to draw strength from Hitler's success in Germany, where in the face of incredible opposition a united, zealous group had eventually rescued an entire nation from disaster. The Bund, he observed, was small in number and financially weak; yet through sacrifice and determination it could overcome the cowardice and laziness of the majority of German-Americans and restore the prestige they had lost during World War I. He believed that "the Judaicized, so-called British

Empire" would soon be defeated. Upon the ashes of that defeat a new Aryan America would be built. In subsequent weeks Kunze continually made similar appeals to Bundists to find inspiration in Hitler's achievements. In his 1940 Christmas greeting to the membership he praised Hitler for elevating the German people to their highest level of power and prestige. Hitler's accomplishment of uniting people of German blood provided a model for German-Americans that would give courage and faith to all Bundists in the "coming battle-year 1941." Kunze's year-end message to Bund youth members philosophized on the sufferings of 1940 when, he claimed, German-American children were insulted and ridiculed at school and on the streets. He told the young people to stand firm, remain loyal to their blood, and take hope from the perseverance Germany and the German people had displayed in the past year.[15]

The call for greater dedication may have helped bolster morale, but it could not solve the Bund's practical problems of insolvency and insubordination. Kunze complained that his Commands requiring members and units to replenish Bund finances were treated with indifference. A series of difficult legal problems persisted. Although the Nordland case, charging several Bundists with violating a race-hatred law, as well as the Chicago tax case remained in abeyance, Kuhn's attorney, Peter Sabbatino, had initiated a suit against Kunze for failing to pay for services rendered during Kuhn's trial. Another suit, involving ownership of a Brooklyn meeting hall, was being prepared for court. This case resulted from the refusal of a pro-Kuhn group to relinquish Bund property to Kunze. At the same time the Bund lost two important leaders: Western Gau Leader Herman Schwinn had his American citizenship revoked on the grounds of a forged entry in his naturalization papers; and Hans Diebel, manager of the Aryan Book Store, suffered the same fate on the allegation that promoting Nazi literature was not fitting to an American citizen.[16]

Beginning in the spring of 1941, a series of events occurred which virtually sealed the organization's fate. In effect the Bund was harassed out of existence. A California un-American activities committee opened an investigation of the Bund; Florida enacted a statute outlawing the organization in the Sunshine State; a Dies Committee report, made public in May, gave a complete indictment of the Bund as a Nazi agency. On May 30 New Jersey Attorney General David T.

Wilnetz ordered local enforcement officers to close Camp Nordland. A few days later Governor Charles Edison signed a bill, passed unanimously by the New Jersey legislature, revoking the charter and incorporation of the German-American Bund Auxiliary, the owner of Nordland. When the Auxiliary tried to evade the law by transferring its title to 217 individuals known collectively as the Nordland Home Owners Association, the camp was seized and placed in the custody of the State of New Jersey. Other actions struck at the American Nazi movement. In June President Roosevelt included Bund funds in a general order freezing Axis assets in the United States. Soon afterward federal tax liens were filed against the Bund, and a New York legislative committee began an investigation to determine the Bund's influence in the public schools.[17]

By the summer of 1941 the Bund could no longer hold public meetings. To avoid violence and harassment, local units often masqueraded as singing or gymnastic societies. One unit leader whimsically commented, "We have learned how to sing." The OD became an athletic organization. Members were advised to stop using the fascist salute and to avoid uniforms and flag displays. Kunze seemed most concerned about the possible collapse of the *Free American*. After announcing that the paper would be reduced from twelve to six pages, he asked each member to purchase an extra year's subscription. Members of Kunze's staff were threatening resignation because units ignored dues payments. In the face of circumstances so adverse, Kunze could only beseech members not to yield "to these last attempts to subjugate us."[18]

In early November, Kunze suddenly fled to Mexico. The executive committee immediately met in special session to formally depose him and to appoint Mid-West Gau Leader George Froboese as acting national leader. Units were informed that Kunze was dismissed on grounds of incompetence. Froboese tried to rally the disoriented members by affirming the absolute righteousness of the Bund's cause. Kunze had lost confidence in the movement's future; in the course of the organization's history others lacking physical and spiritual strength had also fallen, but the new Bundesführer argued that the sacrifices of Bundists were insignificant when compared to those of German soldiers fighting against Bolshevism. Members had only one duty, which fate had destined for them—to preserve this movement based on sacred German blood.[19]

Froboese's effort was in vain. The end for the Bund came on the day after Pearl Harbor, when the executive committee unanimously adopted a motion to disband the organization. Three days later, on December 11, 1941, the United States declared war on the Axis powers, and Treasury Department agents raided Bund national headquarters and seized all records. Important Bund officials were immediately taken into custody by federal authorities. Kunze was picked up in Mexico and returned to the United States; he received a fifteen-year prison sentence for engaging in subversive activities. George Froboese and a few lesser-known Bundists committed suicide. Twenty-four Bund officials were convicted of conspiracy to violate the 1940 Selective Service Act. Kunze along with Herman Schwinn, August Klapprott, and Hans Diebel were defendants in the famous sedition case, United States vs. McWilliams. Some Bundists had their naturalized citizenship revoked and spent a few months in detention camps. Fritz Kuhn lost his citizenship and was deported to Germany after 1945. Most Bund members, however, were not unduly harassed. During the war a few spy cases involving ex-Bundists created sensational news copy but proved nothing about the activities and loyalties of the mass of Bundists.[20]

NOTES

1. *Times*, March 3, April 1, May 18, 26, 27, 1939; "Woes of a Führer."
2. *Weckruf*, May 11, 18; June 1, 8, 29; July 6, 1939; *Statement of National Leader Fritz Kuhn of the German-American Bund*, June 1, 1939, in RG 131, Box 159; *Minutes of the National Convention of the German-American Bund*, July 2, 3, 1939, in RG 131, Box 145; *Times*, August 17, 18; September 30, October 1, 4, 5, 6, 7, 8, 9, 12, 19, 20, 26; November 2, 1939; *German Americans! All Americans! Stand Up Against Persecution, Mayor LaGuardia, Thomas E. Dewey, Martin Dies and to whom it may concern*, in RG 131, Box 47. The $50,000 bail came chiefly from donations and loans of members and sympathizers in the New York area. The largest loan was $3500 and highest gift $1000. The Union City, New Jersey, Bund unit collected the money and Bundist August Klapprott, who managed the collection, claimed that thousands of people had sent contributions. See *Times*, October 22, 1939.
3. For a complete transcript of the testimony, proceedings, and exhibits of the trial, see RG 131, Boxes 48 and 49; the *Times* gave excellent coverage of the trial; See November 10-December 6, 1939. Dewey's role in prosecuting Kuhn is briefly discussed in Hughes, *Attorney for the People*, pp. 334-336.

4. Arthur Smith, *The Deutschtum of Nazi Germany,* pp. 107-112, 117-151; Frye, *Nazi Germany* p. 92; Arthur Smith, "The Kameradschaft USA." Many members of Kameradschaft USA experienced difficulties and frustrations in regaining their German citizenship. After the German attack on the Soviet Union, Kameradschaft units became part of a plan to resettle Poland with Germans. Some months later the retreat of German armies from Russia led to abandonment of the program.

5. *Weckruf,* December 7, 14, 21, 28, 1939; *Statement of the German-American Bund Regarding the Indictment, Trial and So-Called Conviction of Fritz Kuhn,* December 11, 1939, in RG 131, Box 159; Letter of G. Wilhelm Kunze to Fritz Kuhn, December 18, 1939, in RG 131, Box 204; *Junges Volk,* December 1939, January 1940; *Minutes of the Special Meeting of the Executive Committee of the German-American Bund,* December 6, 1939, in RG 131, Box 16.

6. Bund Command No. 25, November 30, 1939; No. 26, December 15, 1939; No. 27, January 12, 1940; No. 27-A, January 15, 1940; *German-American Bund Organizational Structure and Rules and Regulations for Officers and Members,* February 1, 1940, in RG 131, Box 16.

7. *Minutes of the National Convention of the German-American Bund,* August 31-September 1, 1940, in RG 131, Box 2.

8. Ibid.; Bund Command No. 28, February 15, 1940; No. 28-A, February 15, 1940; No. 29, March 10, 1940; No. 30, April 6, 1940; No. 31, April 24, 1940; No. 32, May 15, 1940; No. 33, June 20, 1940.

9. *Statement of the German-American Bund,* September 7, 1939, in RG 131, Box 159; Bund Command No. 23, September 8, 1939; *Free American,* February 8, 15, 21, 29, 1940; *George Washington's Birthday,* official Bund program, in RG 131, Box 143. The name of the Bund newspaper became *The Free American* with the January 7, 1940, issue. See Frye, *Nazi Germany,* p. 96, for a good listing of the themes emphasized by Nazi propagandists in thier efforts to mold American opinion during the period of neutrality, 1939-1941.

10. Telegrams and letters of G. Wilhelm Kunze to President Roosevelt and Vice President Garner, September 12, 15, 1940, in RG 131, Box 147; Bund Command No. 37, October 1, 1940.

11. *Free American,* January 30, February 13, March 20, 1941. Willkie repudiated anti-Semitic, undemocratic groups which announced support of his candidacy and he denounced Nazi Germany. Unfortunately he took the brunt of a rancorous anti-Nazi campaign which spread cheap pulp literature claiming that a vote for Willkie was a vote for Hitler. See Goodrich, "Politics and Prejudices"; Bone, *Smear Politics: An Analysis of 1940 Campaign Literature.* The Bund correctly perceived the depth of anti-Roosevelt sentiment in the German-American community. The German-American vote went to Willkie in 1940 in protest against Roosevelt's foreign policies. See Gerson, *The Hyphenate in Recent American Politics,* pp. 123-131; Brown and Roucek (eds.), *One America,* pp. 421-422. The German government made a massive propaganda effort to defeat Roosevelt which significantly ignored the Bund. See Frye, pp. 152-167.

12. Bund Command No. 41, January 20, 1941; No. 42, February 15, 1941; *Free American,* May 1, 8, 29, 1941; Cole, *America First: The Battle Against Intervention, 1940-1941,* pp. 117-119, 122; Johnson, *The Battle Against Isolation,* pp. 147-161.

13. Cantril, "America Faces the War: A Study in Public Opinion," pp. 395, 401; Cantril, Rugg, and Williams, "America Faces the War: Shifts in Opinion"; DeJong, *The German Fifth Column,* pp. 21-25, 105-107; "Nazi Agents in the U.S."; Cranston, "Congress and the Alien"; Goodrich, "Nazi Interference in American Affairs"; Biddle, *In Brief Authority,* pp. 106-119; *Times,* September 11, 14, 16, December 20, 21, 1940; "Foreign Language Press"; "Digest of Magazine Opinion."

14. Lawyers briefs on this case in RG 131, Box 27. See also *Times,* August 19, 20, 23, 1940; *Free American,* August 1, 15, 1940; Handbills advertising the meeting and Kuhn appeal leaflets, in RG 131, Box 90.

15. *Minutes of the National Convention of the German-American Bund,* August 31-September 1, 1940, in RG 131, Box 2; Bund Command No. 39, December 15, 1940; *Junges Volk,* December 1940.

16. Bund Command No. 38, November 19, 1940; No. 39, December 15, 1940; No. 40, January 5, 1941; No. 43, March 26, 1941; *Minutes of the German-American Bund Executive Committee,* March 31, 1941, in RG 131, Box 16.

17. Barrett, *The Tenney Committee,* pp. 11-14; *Times,* April 23, May 24, 25, 31, June 9, 10, 11, 17, August 18, 1941; Certificate of Dissolution signed by the Trustees of the German-American Auxiliary, Inc., in RG 131, Box 26; Subpoena to German-American Bund from Joint Legislative Committee to Investigate the Educational System of the State of New York, July 22, 1941, in RG 131, Box 200.

18 Bund Command No.44, June 20, 1941; No.45, July 5, 1941; *Minutes of the National Convention of the German-American Bund,* August 30-31, 1941, in RG 131, Box 2.

19. Rogge, *Official German Report,* p. 115; *Minutes of a Special Meeting of the German-American Bund Executive Committee,* November 13, 1941; Bund Command No. 49, November 13, 1941; No. 50, December 2, 1941.

20. *Minutes of the German-American Bund Executive Committee,* December 8, 1941; Rogge, *Official German Report,* p.129; *Times,* December 16, 1941; *Bund,* pp. 3-5; Myers, *History of Bigotry in the United States,* pp. 340-342; *Contemporary Jewish Record,* V, August 1942, p. 422; October 1942, p. 522; Biddle, pp. 239-295; Rachlis, *They Came To Kill.*

7

NEO-NAZIS

In May 1945 National Socialist Germany collapsed, exploding in blood and flame under the blows of the Allied armies. Hitler and many leaders of the Third Reich were dead; a few faced charges of war crimes and were brought to judgment before an international tribunal; and some fled Germany to live underground in the Middle East and in Latin America. The threat of Nazism to America and the world appeared to be eliminated. Yet within a decade after World War II fanatical neo-Nazis sprouted up in Germany, England, the Middle East, South Africa, Latin America, and the United States. This Nazi revival, while small and not overtly organized, seemed ominous to those who remembered that Hitler, too, had begun with a tiny group of devoted followers.[1]

In the United States the postwar years saw a tremendous proliferation of radical right-wing societies.[2] This far-right fringe consisted of many fascist-type groups such as the Ku Klux Klan, the National States' Rights Party, and the John Birch Society; but only one group, the American Nazi Party, openly identified itself with Adolf Hitler and National Socialism. The founder of the American neo-Nazi movement, George Lincoln Rockwell, was born on March 9, 1918, in Bloomington, Illinois, the son of "Old Doc" Rockwell, a popular vaudeville and radio comedian of the 1920's and 1930's. There were no unusual events in his early life to account for his later attraction to Nazism. Although his parents' divorce forced George as a child to live alternately with his mother in Illinois and his father in Maine, he was given every educational opportunity. He attended Hebron Academy, a prep school in Maine, and in 1938 went to Brown University to major in philosophy. At both institutions he showed more interest in commercial art than in the liberal arts. His academic life ended abruptly in 1941, when he left the university to join the Navy. In his autobiography, *This Time the World*, Rockwell attributes his participation in the war effort against Germany to youthful political naiveté and to the anti-Hitler propaganda which made him believe that Nazism represented a mortal threat to the United States. This judgment ignores the fact that he earned a good war record flying antisubmarine missions over the South Atlantic and South Pacific and was discharged with the rank of lieutenant commander.[3]

Rockwell's return to civilian life in 1945 marked the end of his normal life pattern; hereafter he experienced a series of failures and frustrations. His first marriage ended in divorce, and he tried without success to pursue a career in commercial art. With the outbreak of the Korean war in 1950 he was recalled to active military duty and received assignments to San Diego and later to Iceland. Although the Navy restored order and discipline to his life, the Commander underwent a profound psychological change at this time. The transformation began when he was introduced to the world of anti-Semitism by an unnamed acquaintance who guided him to anti-Jewish tabloids and the anti-Communist speeches of Senator Joseph McCarthy. His interest was so intense that in his off-duty hours he went to the San Diego Public Library to gather material from Jewish newspapers and government documents. He read *The Protocols of the Wise Elders of Zion* and commented that it was written by a genius who accurately analyzed world Jewry's devious history and ultimate goals. He became obsessed with a desire to fight Jews but lacked a philosophical framework from which he could launch an attack.[4] A reading of *Mein Kampf* gave him that ideology. He studied, reread, and underlined its important passages and was converted to National Socialism. Hitler's book deeply impressed him:

> In *Mein Kampf* I found abundant "mental sunshine," which bathed all the gray world suddenly in the clear light of reason and understanding. Word after word . . . stabbed into the darkness like thunderclaps and lightningbolts

of revelation, . . . I was transfixed, hypnotized. I could not lay the book down without agonies of impatience to get back to it.[5]

In 1952 the Navy transferred Rockwell to Iceland, where he continued to study all available anti-Semitic and Nazi literature. Here he met his second wife, and the couple honeymooned at Berchtesgaden, Hitler's favorite retreat. A few years later this marriage, like the first one, was terminated by divorce.[6]

After his discharge from active military service in 1954 Rockwell tasted persistent failure. He started a monthly magazine, *U. S. Lady*, for wives of servicemen which covertly presented his political views. It failed. Next he established an association called The American Federation of Conservative Organizations, which faded away almost as soon as it was formed. By this time his savings were exhausted, and he tried working for a variety of conservative causes and enterprises. Because he had difficulty subordinating himself to others, Rockwell could not function well in a normal job situation. He wanted to dominate people, and when this urge was frustrated, a job became intolerable. As he drifted from one job to another, seeking a place for himself, the Commander became disenchanted with traditional rightist groups and politicians. Despondent and rejected, he withdrew into a private, unreal world, where he mapped plans for an underground Nazi movement. He later wrote of a recurring dream which helped sustain him during these difficult times: he would be busy at work or walking through a crowded lobby or sitting in a theatre when he would be approached and told that there was someone to see him. The dream ended with Rockwell's walking to a back office, opening the door, and meeting Adolf Hitler alone inside. Like an old-time fundamentalist who anticipates a religious calling, he considered this dream a summons to continue the Führer's work. Rockwell assumed that by becoming "an open, arrogant, all-out Nazi" he would attract attention, win support, and clearly distinguish himself from the right, which in his opinion consisted of "cowards, nuts, one-track minds, blabbermouths, boobs, incurable tight-wads, and—worst of all—hobbyists." One rightist, Harold N. Arrowsmith, Jr., a wealthy businessman who shared Rockwell's sentiments, apparently did not fit this category. Arrowsmith was unable to publish his articles, which purported to show Jewish intrigues in past historical events. Determined to see his works in print, Arrowsmith decided to publish them himself. He met Rockwell, and their mutual interests led the two men to create The National Committee to Free America from Jewish Domination. Arrowsmith provided Rockwell with printing equipment and a house at Arlington, Virginia. But the sharp, hostile public reaction to the anti-Jewish demonstrations Rockwell conducted led Arrowsmith to withdraw his support, and the partnership ended. The Commander persevered and in March 1959 he named the movement the American Nazi Party.[7]

In his two-story frame house at Arlington, just a ten-minute drive across the Potomac River from the White House, Rockwell established the national headquarters of the American Nazi Party. The building is an unimposing run-down structure, which attracts attention only because of the large wooden swastika fastened to the gable in the center of the roof. Wire mesh protects all the windows. Often a sign hangs on the porch reading, "White Man Fight! Smash the Black Revolution!" The doormat is a Jewish altar cloth, and inside there is a shrine dedicated to Adolf Hitler. In this room portraits of Adolf Hitler, George Washington, and George Lincoln Rockwell flank a huge spotlighted silk Nazi flag hanging in the center of a black wall. Another spotlight shines on a bust of Hitler, mounted on a pedestal, while on a center table a candle burns perpetually in honor of imprisoned party members. Party literature is stacked near a scroll, designed by Rockwell, which lists the names of members who have taken an oath against consuming cigarettes and alcoholic beverages. For many years the party mascot, a Doberman named Gas Ovens, guarded the premises.[8]

From national headquarters Rockwell controlled an organization of a few hundred members and sympathizers, with units in Dallas, Texas; Los Angeles, San Francisco, and Oakland, California; Chicago, Illinois; Boston, Massachusetts; and Arlington and Spotsylvania, Virginia. The individuals who joined the movement had several common traits. They were young, in their early and mid-twenties, and came from a lower-middle-class background; often they were products of broken homes. A few attended college. They were prone to violence, always eager to use their fists to settle a dispute, and many had criminal or prison records for minor offenses of theft, vagrancy, or disorderly conduct. Some had seen military service in the army or marine corps; all intensely disliked Jews and Blacks. To capture new members, the party distributed recruitment propaganda which made its appeal in crude black-and-white racial terms, calling upon "young white men" to take the offensive against "the black menace" by joining the American Nazi Party.[9]

An individual who joins the party takes an oath:

> In the presence of the Great Spirit of the Universe and my loyal Party comrades, I hereby irrevocably pledge: To Adolf Hitler, the philosophical leader of the White Man's fight for an idealistic and scientific world order against the atheistical and materialistic forces of Marxism and racial suicide, I pledge my reverence and respect. To the Commander of Adolf Hitler's National Socialist Movement, I pledge my faith, my courage, and my obedience. To my Party Comrades, throughout the world, I pledge my absolute loyalty, even unto death. To myself, as a leader of the White Man's fight, I pledge a clean and manly life of honor. To the United States of America, I pledge my loyalty and my careful compliance with its Constitution and laws until those which are unjust can be legally changed by winning the hearts of the people. To my ignorant fellow white men, who will hate and persecute me because they have been so cruelly brainwashed, I pledge my patience and my love. To the traitors of my race and nation, I pledge swift and ruthless justice.[10]

This oath is the initiation into an organization operating on paramilitary lines, with the national commander acting as Führer. He determines policy, makes the important decisions, and is aided by "majors," "captains," and "lieutenants." Group and storm leaders command the storm troopers, the lowest echelon of the movement. The official uniform of the American Nazi storm trooper is khaki shirt and trousers, paratrooper boots, fatigue cap, and swastika arm band. Storm troopers engage in physical training exercises, receive weapons instructions, and hold military drills, but their main duties are picketing and distributing leaflets at demonstrations, printing party publications, and serving as bodyguards to the Commander. They are indoctrinated with Nazi values, told to cooperate with the FBI and the police, and above everything else taught that party loyalty is the supreme virtue. To encourage loyalty and maintain a military atmosphere, the party holds ceremonies at national headquarters at which storm troopers receive awards and medals such as the "Medal of Merit" or the "Order of Adolf Hitler" for their "heroic action" at demonstrations.[11]

In July 1960 the American Nazi Party vaulted into national attention when police quelled a riotous disturbance on the National Mall and Rockwell was committed to St. Elizabeth's Hospital, in Washington, D. C., for psychiatric observation. This experience

prompted him to write a pamphlet, *How To Get Out or Stay Out of the Insane Asylum*, in which he explained the reason for his confinement and outlined how he secured his discharge. Rockwell saw himself as a victim of a Jewish conspiracy; he believed that Jews, alarmed over his political views, wanted to eliminate his influence by incarcerating him in an insane asylum. To defeat this plot and to manipulate psychiatry—a science based on "Jew Freud's ideas"— Rockwell devised guidelines for winning his freedom. The first rule was to cooperate with everyone—inmates, doctors, nurses, guards— with the aim of avoiding any act of violence. A second advised positive responses to the Rorschach test: one should see and talk about pleasant things, not blood, bodies, or wreckage. A third rule was to recognize that the Jewish conspiracy was not all-embracing, that there were honest men, even some "good Jews," who were ignorant of the "deadly plot of top Jew-Communist-Zionists." Rockwell cited examples of "sincere" doctors who were convinced of his sanity and worked for his release. A final rule was never to refuse medication or treatment prescribed by doctors, because hesitation or resistance to taking a pill or an injection might encourage staff observers to declare you insane. Rockwell's guidelines proved successful. In August 1960 the psychiatrists declared him sane, although he was diagnosed a paranoid personality. He stood trial, received a $100 fine for disorderly conduct, and returned to party affairs.[12]

One of Rockwell's great dreams was the unification of all National Socialist movements into a worldwide federation, a project which consumed much of his time and energy in the early years of the American Nazi Party. Such a union was, in his view, an absolute prerequisite for "the survival of the White Race." This conviction was based on Rockwell's interpretation of Western civilization, which, he argued, had passed its zenith in the nineteenth century and had degenerated into an effete, cowardly culture devoid of its former heroic qualities and concerned only with humanitarianism and a love of ease and luxury. In the twentieth century, however, a unique historical event—the appearance of Adolf Hitler—offered an opportunity to reverse this suicidal trend. Hitler tried to salvage a "Jewized, cannibalized, and boobized civilization," and although his movement was thwarted by the "Jewish forces of decay and destruction," its very existence and contemporary revival proved that the West still had creative potential. Today, Rockwell argued, Western civilization faced its greatest threat, and only a revitalized National Socialist movement organized along international lines could success-fully cope with it. The American Führer saw the danger in these terms: in their bid for total world domination, Jews had used the ploy of divide and rule, manipulating white nations into fratricidal wars and frenzied states of nationalism. In the final stage of their conquest Jews now used a new and deadlier strategy—mobilizing all non-Caucasian peoples into a violent mass movement against the West. A ruthlessly executed racial counter-revolution, Rockwell be-lieved, inspired by the common goals, symbols, and heroes National Socialism provided for all white men, would save the West and permit white elites, the true culture creators, to flourish for another thousand years.[13]

In the summer of 1962 Rockwell went to England to bring his dream of worldwide Nazi federation closer to reality. Barred from the country by the British government, he eluded the authorities with the aid of British National Socialist leader Colin Jordan, who smuggled him to a Nazi camp gathering held at Dead-and-Bury Hollow near Temple Guiting, Gloucestershire, about 130 miles west of London. There, at a dramatic night rally encircled with torches and honor guards, Rockwell spoke about "criminal Jew Communism, race-mixing, and subversion" and "our mighty Nazi movement." Eventually the meeting at Dead-and-Bury Hollow produced a mani-festo called the Cotswold Agreement which established the World Union of National Socialists (WUNS). Delegates from Great Britain, the United States, Germany, Austria, France, the Irish Republic, and Belgium ratified the agreement, pledging themselves to battle against world Jewry, to work for an international apartheid policy which would specify areas of the world where each race would dominate and be separated from all others, and finally, to complete a world-wide "final settlement of the Jewish problem." Colin Jordan became the first World Führer of this organization, which sought to unite all Nazi parties. Later, with his imprisonment, the leadership passed to Rockwell, who continued to make his residence at Arlington, the international Nazi headquarters. Party publications gave WUNS a great amount of attention: in *The Stormtrooper* Rockwell wrote that this "Internationale of the White Man" held the winning strategy in the struggle against Jewish Communism by providing Caucasians everywhere with a new sense of racial unity, loyalty, and destiny;

recruiting advertisements called upon "white peoples of the World" to "unite and fight"; news items reported on Jewish anxiety over the increased growth and influence of WUNS. WUNS published a journal, *National Socialist World*, which appeared irregularly and was written in a pseudoscholarly style. It featured articles on Nazi racial policies, reports on Nazis harassed for their beliefs, and documentaries detailing the history of events important to National Socialism.[14]

On the domestic scene Rockwell employed shock tactics to capture mass-media exposure. Publicity for the party became his main objective, and one effective means of winning that goal was an arrogant display of the swastika. He believed that it attracted courageous, fighting, race-conscious young men who were Nazis by instinct. More significant was the debilitating effect of the swastika on Jews. Upon seeing it, he argued, Jews lost their cold, calculating reasoning abilities and became hysterical, screaming with fear and rage at the American Nazi Party. This reaction led Jews to unwittingly aid the movement: while moving to stamp out Nazism, they were forced to give the party free publicity through their TV, press, and magazine agencies. The Commander also saw the swastika as a symbol capable of rallying the masses. Like Hitler, he believed that the masses represented the submissive, eager to be dominated "eternal female," who could never be influenced by reasoned arguments. The masses were always swayed by force and strength; and a powerful, brazen Nazi movement, symbolized by the swastika, would have an irresistible appeal to their unsophisticated minds.[15]

In his quest for publicity Rockwell staged noisy and startling demonstrations timed to coincide with controversial events in order to insure TV or press attention. A dramatic example occurred in 1961 when, in response to the freedom rides of civil-rights workers, he sent into the South a group of Nazis in a Volkswagen bus covered with signs reading: "Lincoln Rockwell's Hate Bus," "We Hate Race-Mixing," and "We Hate Jew Communism." Agitation against civil-rights activities became a party tradition, with storm trooper picket squads parading in front of the White House, at NAACP conventions, and at integration marches, where they displayed anti-Negro signs, waved swastikas, and chanted "White Power." The movie *Exodus*, a story of Israel's struggle for nationhood, and the play *The Deputy*, a condemnation of Pope Pius XII's policies toward Jews during World War II, brought out the Nazis, who emerged with pickets just before showtime. At antiwar rallies storm troopers appeared to rip down Viet Cong flags and throw paint, eggs, beer cans, and garbage at the "peace creeps."[16] Almost every Nazi demonstration ended with a violent confrontation between storm troopers and enraged onlookers. Arrests followed and the Nazis were charged with disorderly conduct. But bruised fists, cut faces, small fines, and short jail sentences were small prices for the storm troopers to pay for receiving news coverage.

As the party reaped more and more press notices, Rockwell capitalized on its growing notoriety by accepting invitations to speak at colleges and universities. Between 1962 and 1964 students heard him on numerous campuses, including San Diego State College, Carleton College, Hofstra University, George Washington University, American University, Colorado State University, and the Universities of Chicago, Virginia, Maryland, Colorado, Minnesota, and Kansas. His appearances drew large crowds, making headline stories in local newspapers, and often he was interviewed on TV or radio stations. The Commander relished this opportunity to spread his message and saw it as a countermeasure against "Jewish, Communist, Zionist, race-mixing propaganda."[17]

Rockwell's speaking engagements earned important contributions to the party's finances, a subject he rarely discussed. Occasionally he told newsmen that several "fat cats," who wished to remain anonymous, stood ready to subsidize American Nazism. But these individuals were either nonexistent or extremely reluctant to extend aid, for the party never prospered. Its continued calls for individual contributions, food, blankets, silverware, and stamps indicated a weak financial condition. The movement's main source of income appeared to come from the sale of party publications, photographs, movies, tapes, and varied Nazi paraphernalia. Among the publications were Rockwell's autobiography, *This Time the World*; the official party magazine, *The Stormtrooper; The Stormtrooper's Manual*; a number of Rockwell's pamphlets, notably *In Hoc Signo Vinces* and *How To Get Out or Stay Out of the Insane Asylum*; and an assortment of leaflets called Rockwell Reports, which included such titles as *Analysis of Jew Techniques for Destroying the White South, Analysis of Facts on Kosher Conservatives, Analysis of Jew Techniques in Destroying Gentile Character, Analysis of Jew Leadership of Sheep-Like Masses,* and *Laughable Exposé of Jew Ostrich Silent Treatment of*

Nazis. There were other popular leaflets: *Peace Creeps, Nigger—You Too Can Be a Jew*, and *Proof that Goldwater is a Plant*. Advertisements in *The Stormtrooper* promoted a variety of "hell-raising" items. A "Jew traitor's surrender pass" promised a late gassing to a Jew who confessed treasonous activity. A "boat ticket to Africa" offered a one-way trip to the Dark Continent to any Black. A 45-rpm "Hatenany Record" featured Odis Cochran and the "musical prejudice of the 3 bigots," singing the songs "Ship Those Niggers Back" and "We is Nonviolent Niggers." There were swastika-decorated gummed stickers with blunt slogans—"Race-Mixing is Jewish," "Communism is Jewish," "Death to Traitors," "Liberate Jew-Occupied New York," and "Hitler was Right."¹⁸ These inflammatory, provocative items represented Rockwell's handiwork. He had a talent for coining a shocking phrase, and his training in commercial art gave him the technical skill for illustrating the party's publications with lurid, tasteless artwork.

Other materials turned out by the party included photographs of Hitler and Rockwell, 8-mm color movies of American Nazi marches and rallies, an American Nazi calendar, tapes of Rockwell's speeches, "White Power" T shirts, and a bust of Adolf Hitler. A collection of Nazi furnishings was advertised: swastika banners and arm bands, eagle and swastika hat and lapel pins, a death's-head medallion with chain, the official NSDAP pin, and eagle-and-swastika cuff links. Finally, standard anti-Semitic literature received publicity: *Mein Kampf* by Adolf Hitler, *The International Jew* by Henry Ford, *The Inequality of Human Races* by Arthur de Gobineau, *Judaism in Music* by Richard Wagner, and *The Protocols of the Wise Elders of Zion* were but a few of the titles.

The basic theme emerging from the literature of the American Nazi Party is a fusion of anti-Negro with anti-Jewish sentiment. All of the evil characteristics the Nazis attributed to Jews were applied equally to Blacks. They, like Jews, were referred to as "scum," "plague," "filth," "beasts," "rats," "animals," and "inferior creatures" and were seen as disruptive elements out to destroy America by breaking down the will of the white, Gentile majority. Although Jews represented the greater threat since they held controlling positions in every facet of American society, Blacks were also dangerous because their "low animal-nature" made them prone to violence. Party literature presented the two ethnic groups working together in elections to vote the best "race-mixing" candidate into office and also depicted Jews manipulating Blacks into acts of rape, looting, and arson by means of civil-rights organizations and the promotion of Communist propaganda. The Nazis proposed several ways of challenging this reputed Jewish-Black threat to the United States. One remedy lay in violence. Two editorials by Rockwell in *The Stormtrooper* entitled "Terrorism the Only Answer to Terrorism" and "When They Burn Our Flag Its Time for Violence" ranted against "Black terrorists" and Jewish "red rats" and called upon "White men" to arm and fight back in the manner of the Reconstruction Ku Klux Klan.[19] In 1965 the party tried another approach, when Rockwell ran as an independent candidate for the governorship of Virginia. Campaigning against integration, he promised to make every Virginia street safe for white women, to put every white man into the state militia, and to structure Virginia into a model white Christian community. Results of his efforts were dismal: he captured a little over 6,300 votes or 1.2 percent of the total ballots cast.[20] ,

In their efforts to check Jewish and Black activities, the Nazis supported individuals and groups which had aims similar to their own. They warmly complimented General Edwin A. Walker of Dallas, Texas, an outspoken anti-integrationist and advocate of far-right causes. The Black Muslims, partisans of total racial segregation, received Nazi blessings. Rockwell once labeled the Muslim leader, Elijah Muhammed, "the Adolf Hitler of the Black men." At a Chicago Muslim Convention in February 1962 he heaped praise on Elijah, extended the party's support to him, and attacked Jews for exploiting both Blacks and Whites. This friendship soon cooled. The Nazis disapproved of the Muslim demand for an all-Black nation inside the United States. Rockwell's "final solution" for America's race problems was to expel all Jews and Blacks. The former would be eliminated, presumably by gassing in the tradition of the Nazi extermination camps, while all Blacks would be shipped to Africa. This solution, in the Commander's view, would bring peace and prosperity to America.[21]

Rockwell paid a heavy price for being a Nazi. His face was scarred from years of street fighting and forced confrontation. He was subject to repeated depressive mental states over the failure of his movement to capture support. In this morose condition he brooded, slouched about headquarters, and was easily irritated. He was tor-

mented by internal discord among storm troopers, who taunted each
other to the point of violence. Suspicious of conspiracy, he scowled
at dissident members, charging them with treason and disloyalty.
Invariably he spoke to reporters of threats against his life. On August
25, 1967, Rockwell was fatally shot in front of a self-service laundro-
mat at Arlington by John Patler, an editor of *The Stormtrooper* who
had been expelled from the party five months earlier for creating
dissension between dark-haired and blond Nazis. Patler held hardened anti-Jewish and anti-Black sentiments and had begun his own
organization, the American National Party. Its publication, *Kill
Magazine*, promoted murder by bluntly encouraging its readers to kill
their enemies. For acting on this recommendation, Patler received a
twenty-year jail sentence.[22]   Rockwell's death dealt a severe blow to
the American Nazi movement by removing its only effective agitator.
The party had revolved around him, the Commander dominating
every facet of its activities. His death took away the movement's
driving force and left the Nazis without a leader capable of drama-
tizing their controversial views.

Matt Koehl, the party's National Secretary, became the new
American Führer. He was born on January 22, 1935, in Milwaukee,
Wisconsin, served in the Marines, and attended several universities
near his home town. Until Rockwell brought him to Arlington, he
had commanded the party's Chicago unit. Koehl's first concern as
national leader was to dispose of Rockwell's remains, a task which
the former Commander's reputation made extremely difficult. After
Rockwell was denied burial at Arlington National Cemetery, the
Military Cemetery at Culpeper, Virginia, and private cemeteries, he
was cremated and his funeral services were held at party headquarters. In the eulogy Koehl exalted Rockwell for continuing Adolf
Hitler's work and hailed him as a martyr who with wisdom, inspiration, and heroism had guided National Socialism through difficult
years of struggle. The new leader concluded that the best tribute to
the fallen Commander was to emulate his dedication to country and
race. Readers of *The Stormtrooper* were told: "George Lincoln
Rockwell died for you—the White Race."[23]

Rockwell's influence did not end with his death. Many of his
pamphlets, tapes, and his last book, *White Power*, continued to
receive active promotion. *White Power* which represented a summa-
tion of his thought, was advertised as the "American *Mein Kampf*."

The party's format and strategy changed, but the new alterations were presumably the fulfillment of plans Rockwell had formulated in the months before his assassination. The name of the organization became the National Socialist White People's Party (NSWPP), and *The Stormtrooper* was replaced by the bimonthly tabloid *White Power*. More significant was the shift in strategy. Rockwell had interpreted the party's growth and development as a logical, calculated four-phase movement to political power. In the first phase its existence was publicized to the people; the second phase saw the propagation of the party's program; the third dealt with organizing converts; the final phase culminated in the attainment of power, supported by the votes of the masses. The post-Rockwell leadership apparently saw the party in its second and third phases and accordingly developed a strategy focused on refining doctrine and organization.[24]

To define this doctrine, a ten-point program of American National Socialism was published in September 1967, marking the first appearance of a specified set of party aims. At the outset the program reiterated the movement's demand that Blacks be deported and the Jewish influence eliminated. Several of the program's stipulations paralleled the demands of other right-wing extremists: Communism was treason and should be quashed; America should fight wars with the aim of winning total victory by using all available weapons; crime and riots should be "smashed" with immediate force; a man's home, family, and property were sacred; the right to bear arms should not be challenged; free enterprise should be encouraged and protected. Two clauses designed to capture working-class support completed the program—every American should have lifetime economic security, and young people should be given unlimited educational opportunity and aid in establishing a family. In addition to delineating a program, the new leadership emphasized the need for a strong, efficient, and disciplined organization. Ultimately the party aimed at absolute control over the state, and it recognized that a mass movement was required to win that goal. The NSWPP believed that two conditions were necessary before National Socialism would capture a popular following: first, an intense public restlessness, and second, an organization capable of exploiting that crisis situation. To build this organization, the party would mold new recruits into a professional cadre of workers and would expand a new source of finances, the "Official

Supporter Program," in which sympathetic individuals send regular contributions to Arlington headquarters.[25]

In line with the new policy the party staged fewer dramatic publicity events. There were infrequent White House vigils and small demonstrations in support of freeing Rudolf Hess and ending the "treasonous no-win" Vietnam war, but its main effort concentrated on enlarging the membership. A National Socialist Liberation Front (NSLF) was established to enlist high-school and college students. A five-dollar annual fee admitted any white student into this "racial revolutionary organization." In soliciting young people, the Nazis pictured America on the eve of destruction, with decadence and miscegenation rampant. The government was a corrupt system, hopelessly sunk in a mire of unmanageable problems. Lyndon Johnson, Richard Nixon, and George Wallace were tagged Jewish puppets who did not offer solutions to the difficulties rising from campus disorders, racial violence, economic recession, and war. The NSWPP saw Armageddon approaching and was convinced that this final battle would culminate in a new National Socialist order if American youth embraced Aryan values. While appealing to students in apocalyptic terms, the party sought to arouse racial resentments in the white working class. It argued that the "small white wage-earner" faced new discriminations and was exploited by the government's welfare policies. Editorials in *White Power* maintained that whites were excluded from the War on Poverty and were given second preference in job-hiring practices, yet their tax dollars went to a welfare system which gave Blacks a high standard of living and the freedom to riot, along with untold special rights and privileges. To intensify racial animosities, the party newspaper reported lurid stories of the misappropriation of federal funds by Blacks and of Black anti-white violence.[26]

A new feature in the party's ideology was an identification of the movement with revolution. The NSWPP held that there could be no compromise with the existing order. It was "a sick, rotten Jewish abomination" and, if permitted to survive, would ultimately lead to the extinction of the white race. Nor did the party see any conservative or rightist groups offering viable alternatives to the present system; these organizations were controlled by Jews and would not openly admit that race was the issue of our time. The NSWPP stood alone, outside of the American political spectrum, as a unique revolutionary movement determined to destroy the contemporary status quo. In taking this extreme position the Nazis anticipated reprisals: loss of police protection, intimidation and arrest of its members and sympathizers, as well as harassments through other retaliatory measures. Such antagonism would be endured with self-discipline and a conviction that Nazism was the wave of the future. The party expected a showdown sometime in the decade of the 1970's. At that time the great mass of white people would reject their liberal politicians and turn to their only saviors—the determined revolutionary leadership of the NSWPP which would establish a National Socialist state committed to defending and championing the interests of the Aryan race.[27]

Here in the party's strategy and perception of the condition of American society are all the characteristics of the extremist mentality. The Nazis have clearly defined their enemies—Jews, Blacks, Communists, conservatives, liberals, and anyone who ignores race as the cornerstone of civilization. Like the Bundists of the 1930's, they see themselves as a persecuted minority standing at the threshold of a great turning point in history. America's neo-Nazis are convinced that they possess the truth and the methods necessary to redirect society into a new creative, vigorous period. They await a complete and total victory over their adversaries.

NOTES

1. Joesten, "The Menace of Neo-Nazism"; Meskil, *Hitler's Heirs.*
2. Roy, *Apostles of Discord*; U.S. Congress, House, Committee on Un-American Activities, *Preliminary Report on Neo-Fascist and Hate Groups.* For a good analysis of post-World War II far-right movements, see Bell (ed.), *The Radical Right.*
3. Sherwin, *The Extremists*, pp. 151-152; Thayer, *The Farther Shores of Politics*, p. 17; Rockwell, *This Time the World*, p. 17.
4. Pierce, "George Lincoln Rockwell: A National Socialist Life," pp. 16-20; Sherwin, p. 152; Thayer, pp. 17-18
5. Rockwell, *This Time the World*, pp. 154-155.
6. Sherwin, pp. 152-153; Pierce, p. 20.
7. Thayer, pp. 18-20; Sherwin, pp. 153-154: Pierce, pp. 20-28; Rockwell, *This Time the World*, pp. 193-308.
8. *The Stormtrooper*, November 1962; Thayer, pp. 21-22; "Bigot Buildup: Case History of George Lincoln Rockwell," in Newman (ed.), *The Hate Reader*, p. 86; *Newsweek*, LVIII (December 4, 1961), pp. 27-28.

9. *The Stormtrooper*, November 1962, January-February 1964, September-October 1964, January-February 1967; "Bigot Buildup," p. 90; Eisenberg, *The Re-emergence of Fascism*, p. 127. Two stormtroopers won notoriety for their violent acts: Dan Burros, an anti-Semitic Jew and former Ku Klux Klan member, committed suicide after his Jewish background was revealed by the *Times*, and John Patler assassinated Rockwell.

10. Quoted in Rosenthal and Gelb, *One More Victim: The Life and Death of a Jewish Nazi* pp. 84-85. This is a biography of Dan Burros.

11. *National Socialist Bulletin*, January 1961; *The Stormtrooper*, August 1962, January-February 1963, January-February 1964, November 1966; *Official Stormtrooper's Manual*.

12. Rockwell, *How To Get Out or Stay Out of the Insane Asylum*; Rosenthal and Gelb, pp. 115-120.

13. Rockwell, *In Hoc Signo Vinces*.

14. *National Socialist Bulletin*, January 1961; *The Stormtrooper*, November 1962, November-December 1963, November 1966; "Bigot Buildup," pp. 102-104; *National Socialist World*, Numbers 1, 2, 3, 4, 5, and 6.

15. Rockwell, *In Hoc Signo Vinces*.

16. *National Socialist Bulletin*, January 1961, July 1961, September 1961; *The Stormtrooper*, February 1962, August 1962, May-June 1963, September-October 1963, January-February 1964, March 1964, November 1966.

17. *The Stormtrooper*, February 1962, January-February 1963, March 1964; Kansas City *Star*, February 20, 1964.

18. Sherwin, p. 154. Every issue of *The Stormtrooper* advertised the party's publications and paraphernalia.

19. *The Stormtrooper*, Summer 1967.

20. *The Stormtrooper*, November-December 1965; *Times*, July 25, 1965; Thayer, p. 14.

21. *National Socialist Bulletin*, July 1961; *The Stormtrooper*, February 1962, January-February 1963, September-October 1964; Eisenberg, p. 128.

22. *Times*, August 26, 27; October 17; December 16, 17, 1967; *The Stormtrooper*, Summer 1967; Rosenthal and Gelb, pp. 147-151.

23. *Times*, August 28, 29, 30, 31, 1967; *The Stormtrooper*, Autumn 1967.

24. *White Power*, September 1, 1967; *The Stormtrooper*, Autumn 1967; *Official Stormtrooper's Manual*.

25. *White Power*, September 1, 1967; *National Socialist World*, Winter 1967.

26. *Build a New Order; White Power*, June-July 1969, August-September 1969, November-December 1969, January-February 1970, May-June 1970.

27. *White Power*, November-December 1969, January-February 1970; *National Socialist World*, Winter 1968.

8

FAILURE

On the basis of historical experience it appears unlikely that the majority of Americans would ever favor a National Socialist United States. In the nation's past, political movements identified with a foreign country have captured attention but never gained wide support, for in the public eye they have been too closely linked with the country of their origin. The development of American Communism was handicapped by its ties with the Soviet Union, a nation most Americans viewed with distrust and suspicion. A similar impediment thwarted the growth of American Nazism. During the American involvement in World War I, Germanophobia was rampant in the United States; propaganda agencies, notably George Creel's Committee on Public Information, depicted Germans as Huns, beasts, and savages, who specialized in committing brutal atrocities. In the 1930's the activities of American Nazis revived anti-German sentiment. The Friends of the New Germany and the German-American Bund were seen as German imports, alien un-American organizations representing a former enemy. This feeling was particularly strong among veteran groups who struck at the Bund with relentless pressure.

That American Nazism, like its German parent, identified completely with Adolf Hitler aroused animosity. Bundists and neo-Nazis alike have venerated Hitler as a statesman inspired by high ideals and moral principles. His beliefs became religious truths, his decisions the epitome of wisdom. His restoration of Germany to the status of a great power seemed to border on the miraculous and aroused pride in Germans everywhere. But this view was not shared by the majority of Americans. In the 1930's powerful and articulate molders of public opinion, including newspaper editors, church and labor leaders, and liberal politicians, held Hitler responsible for turning Germany into a ruthless police state. During and after World War II he became a symbol of evil, a diabolical man capable of committing any act of human treachery to further his dream of world conquest. Probably no individual in the twentieth century has been so despised by Americans as Adolf Hitler.

The appeal of American Nazism has been limited by the movement's inability to develop a concrete set of attainable goals. Bundists tried unsuccessfully to capture a following by relating the anti-Semitic and anti-Communist themes of German propaganda agencies to American society. By propagating such generalities as the demand for a Gentile-ruled America or the elimination of Jews from the labor movement, they only spun Nazi myths and prejudices. They failed to recognize that American politics is oriented toward pragmatic ends. It responds to concrete pressures and specific proposals; it rarely delves into ideology or projects utopian goals. Rockwell's Nazis attempted to deal with a concrete American problem, the race question, but instead of offering viable solutions, they called for a world federation of Nordic nations to combat the "Black menace." This kind of proselytizing gave the movement an air of unreality and alienated the public.

Nazism in the United States today is a curiosity, an anomaly that decades after the destruction of the Third Reich continues to attract and fascinate a following. But in the troubled atmosphere of contemporary America an extremist group is potentially dangerous and warrants attention. American society is plagued by a cult of violence, race polarization, the alienation of a large segment of youth, and the breakdown of traditional status symbols and authorities. Scorn is directed at the government, encouraging a belief that a new political order of any tenor would be better than the present one. Moderates and radicals engage in bitter dialogue, each displaying a loss of will, a reluctance to exert control over the course of events. A deep malaise penetrates intellectual circles, and prophets of doom and despair find receptive audiences. The likelihood that a small extremist group can exploit these circumstances is doubtful, yet excessive optimism is dampened by the knowledge that powerful political movements in the past originated with fanatics, and in the right situation their program became the consensus of a nation.

BIBLIOGRAPHY

Documents

Documents on German Foreign Policy. Washington, D. C., 1949.

National Archives, Record Group 75, John Collier Papers, German-American Bund file.

National Archives, Record Group 131, APC World War II Seized Records, German-American Bund, Boxes 1-248.

State of New York, *Report of Joint Legislative Committee,* Legislative Document Number 98, 1939.

U.S. Congress, House, Special Committee on Un-American Activities, *Investigation of Nazi and other Propaganda,* Report No. 153, 74th Congress, 1st Sess. 1935.

U.S. Congress, House, Special Committee on Un-American Activities, *Investigation of Un-American Propaganda Activities in the United States, German-American Bund*: Appendix IX, Part IV, 77th Cong., 1st Sess., 1941.

U.S. Congress, House, Special Committee on Un-American Activities, *Preliminary Report on Neo-Fascist and Hate Groups,* December 17, 1954.

U.S. Department of Justice, *German-American Bund. Outline of Evidence,* September 17, 1942.

U.S. Department of Justice, *Minutes of the 1938 National Convention of the German-American Bund.*

Yearbooks

Kämpfendes Deutschtum, Jahrbuch des Amerikadeutschen Volksbundes, New York, 1937, 1938.

128

Newspapers

Deutscher Weckruf und Beobachter, July 5, 1935, to December 11, 1941.
New York *Times,* 1936-1941, 1960-1967.
White Power, 1967-1970.

Books

Barrett, Edward L. Jr. *The Tenney Committee.* Ithaca: Cornell University Press, 1951.
Bell, Daniel, editor. *The Radical Right.* New York: Doubleday & Co., 1963.
Biddle, Francis. *In Brief Authority.* New York: Doubleday & Co., 1962.
Bischoff, Ralph F. *Nazi Conquest Through German Culture.* Cambridge, Mass.: Harvard University Press, 1942.
Bone, Hugh A. *Smear Politics: An Analysis of 1940 Campaign Literature.* Washington, D. C.: American Council on Public Affairs, 1941.
Brown, Francis J., and Roucek, Joseph S., editors. *One America.* New York: Prentice Hall Inc., 1945.
Build a New Order (leaflet). Arlington, Va.: National Socialist Liberation Front, n. d.
Burden, Hamilton T. *The Nuremberg Party Rallies: 1923-1939.* New York: Frederick A. Praeger, 1967.,
Carlson, John Roy. *Under Cover.* New York: E. P. Dutton Co., 1943.
Chamberlain, Lawrence H. *Loyalty and Legislative Action: A Survey of Activity of the New York State Legislature, 1919-1949.* Ithaca, N.Y.: Cornell University Press, 1951.
Cole, Wayne. *America First: The Battle Against Intervention, 1940-1941.* Madison: University of Wisconsin Press, 1953.
Compton, James V. *The Swastika and the Eagle.* Boston: Houghton Mifflin Co., 1967.
Cook, Fred J. *The FBI Nobody Knows.* New York: Pyramid Books, 1965.
Day, Daniel S. "American Opinion Toward National Socialism, 1933-1937." Ph.D. dissertation, University of California, Los Angeles, 1958.
DeJong, Louis. *The German Fifth Column in the Second World War.* Chicago: University of Chicago Press, 1956.
Dies, Martin. *The Trojan Horse in America.* New York: Dodd, Mead & Company, 1940.
Dodd, William E. *Ambassador Dodd's Diary, 1933-1938.* New York: Harcourt, Brace and Co., 1941.
Eisenberg, Dennis. *The Re-emergence of Fascism.* New York: A. S. Barnes & Co., 1967.
Frye, Alton. *Nazi Germany and the American Hemisphere 1933-1941.* New Haven, Conn.: Yale University Press, 1967.
Gellermann, William. *Martin Dies.* New York: The John Day Co., 1944.
Gellhorn, Walter, editor. *The States and Subversion.* Ithaca, N.Y.: Cornell University Press, 1952.
Gerson, Louis L. *The Hyphenate in Recent American Politics and Diplomacy.* Lawrence: University of Kansas Press, 1964.
Hare, William F. *The Brown Network.* New York: Knight Publications, Inc., 1936.

Hawgood, John A. *The Tragedy of German America*. New York: G.P. Putnam's
    Sons, 1940.
Hitler, Adolf. *Mein Kampf*, Boston: Little Brown & Co., 1943.
Hughes, Rupert. *Attorney for the People*. Boston: Houghton Mifflin Co., 1940.
Johnson, Walter. *The Battle Against Isolation*. Chicago: University of Chicago
    Press, 1944.
Jonas, Manfred. *Isolationism in America, 1935-1941*. Ithaca, N.Y.: Cornell
    University Press, 1966.
Kracauer, Siegfried. *From Caligari to Hitler, A Psychological Study of the
    German Film*. New York: Noonday Press, Inc., 1959.
Lavine, Harold. *Fifth Column in America*. New York: Doubleday, Doran and
    Co., 1940.
Ludecke, Kurt G. W. *I Knew Hitler*. New York: Charles Scribner's Sons, 1937.
McGrady, Pat. *Fascism in America* (pamphlet). New York: Jewish Daily Bul-
    letin, 1934.
Meskil, Paul. *Hitler's Heirs*. New York: Pyramid Books, 1961.
Murphy, Raymond E., et al. *National Socialism*. Washington, D. C.: U.S. Govern-
    ment Printing Office, 1943.
Myers, Gustavus. *History of Bigotry in the United States*. New York: Capricon
    Books, 1960.
Newman, Edwin S. editor. *The Hate Reader*. New York: Oceana Publications,
    1964.
Official Stormtrooper's Manual (pamphlet). Arlington, Va.: American Nazi
    Party, 1962.
Ogden, August Raymond. *The Dies Committee*. Washington, D. C.: Catholic
    University of America Press, 1945.
Rachlis, Eugene. *They Came to Kill*. New York: Random House, 1961.
Rauschning, Hermann, *The Voice of Destruction*. New York: G. P. Putnam's
    Sons, 1940.
Rockwell, George Lincoln. *How To Get Out or Stay Out of the Insane Asylum*
    (pamphlet). Arlington, Va: American Nazi Party, 1960.
_____ *In Hoc Signo Vinces* (pamphlet). Arlington, Va.: American Nazi
    Party, 1960.
_____ *This Time the World*. Arlington, Va.: American Nazi Party,
    1963.
_____ *White Power*. Arlington, Va.: American Nazi Party, 1967.
Rogge, O. John. *The Official German Report*. New York: Thomas Yoseloff,
    1961.
Rosenthal, A. M., and Gelb, A. *One More Victim: The Life and Death of a
    Jewish Nazi*. New York: New American Library, 1967.
Roy, Ralph Lord. *Apostles of Discord*. Boston: Beacon Press, 1953.
Sherwin, Mark. *The Extremists*. New York: St.Martin's Press, 1963.
Singer, Kurt D., editor. *Confidential Report on 1036 Pro-Nazi Firms Who
    Believed You Could Do Business with Hitler*. New York: News Background,
    Inc., 1235 Broadway, 1942.
Smith, Arthur L., Jr. *The Deutschtum of Nazi Germany and the United States*.
    The Hague: Martinus Nijhoff, 1965.
Strong, Donald S. *Organized Anti-Semitism in America*. Washington, D.C.:
    American Council on Public Affairs, 1941.
Thayer, George. *The Farther Shores of Politics*. New York: Simon & Schuster,
    1967.

Whitehead, Donald F. *The FBI Story*. New York: Random House, 1956.
Wittke, Carl. *The German Language Press in America*. Lexington: University of Kentucky Press, 1957.
Zeman, Z. A. B. *Nazi Propaganda*. London: Oxford University Press, 1965.

Articles and Periodicals

Belth, Norton, "Problems of Anti-Semitism in the United States," *Contemtemporary Jewish Record*, II, May-June, 1939, 6-19.
Britt, George. "Poison in the Melting Pot," *Nation*, CXLVIII, April 1, 1939, 374-376.
Cantril, Hadley. "America Faces the War: A Study in Public Opinion," *Public Opinion Quarterly*, IV, July 1940, 395-401.
Cantril, Hadley; Rugg, Donald; and Williams, Frederick. "America Faces the War: Shifts in Opinion," *Public Opinion Quarterly*, IV, October 1940, 652.
Contemporary Jewish Record, I, November 1938, 70-71, 72-73; V, August 1942, 340-342. V, October 1942, 522.
Cranston, Alan. "Congress and the Alien," *Contemporary Jewish Record*, III, May-June 1940, 245-252.
Diamond, Sander A. "The Years of Waiting: National Socialism in the United States, 1922-1933," *American Jewish Historical Quarterly*, LIX, March 1970, 256-271.
"Digest of Magazine Opinion," *Contemporary Jewish Record*, IV, February 1941, 76-78.
"Exposing the Bund's Home Ties," *Ken*, II, August 11, 1938, 71.
"Foreign Language Press," *Fortune*,, XXII, November 1940, 90-93, 102-104.
"The German-American Bund Meeting," *Contemporary Jewish Record*, II, March-April 1939, 53-58.
"The Gestapo in the USA," *Ken*, II, 1938, 16-19.
Goodrich, Nathaniel H. "Nazi Interference in America Affairs," *Contemporary Jewish Record*, III, July-August 1940, 370-380.
_____. " Politics and Prejudices," *Contemporary Jewish Record*, III, November-December 1940, 571-576.
Hanighen, Frank C. "Foreign Political Movements in the United States," *Foreign Affairs*, XVI, October 1937, 1-20.
"Heiling Muffled," *Newsweek*, XII, July 25, 1938, 13.
"Hessian Day Rally," *New Republic*, LXXXXVIII, February 22, 1939, 57.
"Imported Nazi Sadism," *Nation*, CXLVI, April 30, 1938, 493.
Jacob, Philip E. "Influences of World Events on U. S. Neutrality Opinion," *Public Affairs Quarterly*, IV, January 1940, 51-52.
Joesten, Joachim. "The Menace of Neo-Nazism," *New Germany Reports*, XV, September 1950.
Kimball, Warren F. "Dieckhoff and America: A German View of German-American Relations, 1937-1941," *The Historian*, XXVII, February 1965, 218-243.
Kris, Ernst. "German Propaganda Instructions of 1933," *Social Research*, IX, February 1942, 46-81.
Lore, Ludwig. "Nazi Politics in America," *The Nation*, CXXXVII, November 29, 1933, 615-617.

Morgan, Barbara S. "Swastika," *Atlantic Monthly*, CIV, February 1935, 143.
National Socialist Bulletin, February 1961-September 1961.
National Socialist World, Vols. I–VI.
"Nazi Agents in the U.S.," *Fortune*, XXII, October 1940, 47-51, 134-148.
"The Nazis are Here," *Nation*, CXLVIII, March 4, 1939, 253.
"Nazi Plague Infects City," *Christian Century*, LV, December 7, 1938, 1513.
"The Nazi Pogroms: Digest of Public Opinion," *Contemporary Jewish Record*, II, January 1939, 41-50.
"New York Nazis Beat Up a Jew at Bund Meeting," *Life*, VI, March 6, 1939 22-23.
"Of Spies and Bund Men," *Nation*, CXLVII, July 2, 1938, 6.
Oliver, Bryce. "Fritz Kuhn Verbatim," *Ken*, IV, May 18 1939, 9-11.
Pierce, William L. "George Lincoln Rockwell: A National Socialist Life," *National Socialist World*, VI, Winter 1967, 13-36.
"Red Indians in Brown Shirts," *New Republic* LXXXXIX, May 17, 1939, 31.
Remak, Joachim. "Friends of the New Germany: The Bund and German-American Relations," *The Journal of Modern History*, XXIX, March 1957, 38-41.
Seligmann, Herbert J. "The New Barbarian Invasion," *New Republic*, LXXXXV, June 22, 1938, 175-177.
Smith, Alson J. "I Went to a Nazi Rally," *Christian Century*, LVI, March 8, 1939, 320-322.
Smith, Arthur L., Jr. "The Kameradschaft USA," *The Journal of Modern History*, XXXIV, December 1962, 398-408.
The Stormtrooper, February 1962-Summer 1967.
Tigner, Hugh S. "Will America Go Fascist?" *Christian Century*, LI, May 2, 1934, 593-594.
"Uncle Sam's Nazis," *Newsweek*, XII, July 18, 1938, 11.
"The War on Isms," *Newsweek*, XII, August 22, 1938, 12.
Weinberg, Gerhard L. "Hitler's Image of the United States," *American Historical Review*, LXIX, July 1964, 1006-1021.
Winner, Percy. "Fascism at the Door," *Scribner's Magazine*, XCIX, January 1936, 33.
"Woes of a Füehrer," *Newsweek*, XIII, June 5, 1939, 12.
"The Yahoos of Yaphank," *Nation*, CXLVII, July 23, 1938, 81.

INDEX